A Town in Conflict

Penarth: The Story

Volume Two

By Phil Carradice

Printed by Beacon Printers(Penarth) Limited.

Contents

Acknowledgements

Thanks must go to the following:-

To the people who so willingly told me the stories of their relations and their part in the history of Penarth. In particular, huge thanks to Pat Edwards, Huw and Kathleen Williams, Joy Hosegood, June Russell, P R James and Janet West.

To those individuals who movingly and easily spoke to me about their experiences in the modern conflicts that have involved Penarth people. Thanks, in particular, to Sam Chick, Elgan Hallett, Ken Howell, Bill Aspinall and Penarth Carpets.

To Alan Thorne for his assistance and advice - supportive and informative as always.

To the staff of Penarth Library, all of them helpful and untiring in their desire to assist with research.

To Marcus Payne of Penarth Library, not just for his support and help, but as a diligent and indefatigable researcher who has, so willingly, placed his own findings at my disposal – without you, Marcus, this would all have taken so much longer

To Julie Oldfield for her work on the census returns for Penarth.

To Steve Ashby for his help with sources regarding the Penarth Police.

To Tony and Anne Hallett of Windsor Bookshop and Penarth Press – more power to your elbow!

Above all, to the people of Penarth, many of whom are no longer with us. Their stories, their lives, are at the core of this book. Without them it would not have been possible.

And finally, as ever, to Trudy, my long-suffering wife – one day, Trudy, I promise to get used to working in the study and not on the dining room table!

Introduction

The story of Penarth has been told many times. So the question has to be asked, why again? The answer is very simple. As a town that did not exist until the middle years of the nineteenth century, the place is a social historian's dream. Due to its short span of existence, with a specific, almost exact moment of creation, it is possible to chart, quite accurately, the rise and fall of buildings, the growth of corporate identity and the development of that delicate but essential structure which goes to make up a living, breathing, vibrant community.

Over the years we have had studies of Penarth's buildings, its docks and pier, its schools and churches, even its gardens and parks. I believe that the time is now ripe to look, in more depth than is usual in studies about the town, at how individual people contributed to its growth. Modern Penarth may have been in existence for less than 200 years but in that time its inhabitants have faced up to, and survived, many problems, difficulties and crises. World war, the closure of the docks that spawned the town in the first place, the Great Depression, strikes – Penarth has endured them all.

Elegant Penarth at the end of the nineteenth century, unprepared for what was to come in the years ahead.

How the people of Penarth responded to the crises in their lives - those delicate moments when their happiness and future prospects, their very existence even, were under sudden threat - makes for a fascinating study, regardless of whether the problems were localized

1

or global in size and significance. This book tries to locate and then catch those moments in time. Taking as its central theme the significant conflicts or wars that have occurred since Penarth came into existence in the years after 1854 and using them as an over-arching structure, it looks unashamedly at people rather than places.

It examines how Penarth celebrated the relief of Ladysmith and Mafeking; it looks at the jingoistic outpourings of emotion during the early days of the First World War; it recounts the adventures of Penarth people during the Spanish Civil War; and it tells the story of the men and women who so willingly joined the forces to defend their country from the threat of Fascism in 1939. Many of the soldiers, men and women alike, did not return from their various wars and are now commemorated on the town's War Memorial. For anyone attempting to look at Penarth people the Memorial is a good place to start.

More than anything else, the book seeks to remember the ordinary man, woman and child in the street, all those unknown but crucially important individuals who helped to form Penarth into the place we know today. Most people are aware of Guy Gibson but very few know about Sam Pearse and Richard Wain, the town's other VC winners. Even fewer can detail the experiences of the Penarth members of 113 Siege Battery. These days almost nobody remembers the name of Emily Ada Pickford, the only Penarth woman to die during the Great War. There are so many more – and their stories deserve to be told.

The range of conflicts seen by the town during its short life span is truly amazing. The Crimean War, the Boer War, the First and Second World Wars, the Korean War, the Falklands conflict and modern day excursions into places like Iraq, Northern Ireland and Afghanistan – Penarth people have served and fought in all of them. And while they were serving, events back home continued apace. The daily grind did not stop but world issues certainly impinged themselves onto the people of Penarth. In many respects their responses were perfectly normal, no different from the people of any other town in Britain. But in other ways they were unique to Penarth – and their responses to the conflicts and crises are what make their stories so compelling.

Remembrance is a difficult emotion to define. Why we remember - and what we remember - are invariably unique to each and every one of us. So why should the men and women killed in war be remembered more than the person knocked down by a double-decker bus?

I think it's because the people lost in war symbolise the sense of community that we all believe to be so important in our lives. It's hard to know what makes a community but it is certainly more than an inward-looking group of individuals who are concerned only with themselves and what they can gain from their short span on this earth. True community is surely about growing together, pulling in the same direction for the greater good.

Communities are not just made up of buildings - public, private, simple or complex. They are comprised mainly of human beings. You can house people in wooden shacks or canvas tents, they will still bond together into a community. And the idea of telling the story of a community through its people – in adversity, in triumph, through failure, through success – has to appeal to any historian and writer.

The railway brought prosperity to the town, in the shape of coal for the docks and tourists for the pier and Esplanade.

The book does not just tell the story of Penarth's casualties. While the town has had over 600 people killed in the various wars, countless more enlisted, served and survived. And this is their story, just as much as it is the story of those who did not come back at the end of conflict. It is the story of those who fought and those who stayed at home. It is the story of a town, a community, told through the lives of its people.

Hopefully, the book will be a welcome addition to the story of a unique town.

Phil Carradice, August 2006

The twin elements that created 'penarth - the docks & the beach.

4

Chapter One – The Early Years.

As most people know, the town of Penarth did not exist until the middle years of the nineteenth century. In 1855 Robert Clive, of the Windsor-Clive family at St Fagan's, became chairman of the company formed to build a coal exporting harbour on the River Ely. At that time the population of Penarth village - or hamlet as it might be better termed - stood at just under 500. And that figure included the three separate parishes of Penarth, Llandough and Cogan. These were the parishes that soon came to form the "new town" of Penarth and in 1855 the predominant employment in the area can be termed "agricultural." Within the space of a few short years things began to change dramatically.

With the creation of the tidal harbour and, subsequently, of Penarth Dock itself people came flocking to the area. Almost overnight the place was transformed from a rural to an urban environment and for the years leading up to the opening of the docks – and, indeed, for several years afterwards - the primary employment for men in the town was that of excavator or labourer. Use of the word "town" is appropriate for the new community in these early years. Workmen needed somewhere to live and whole streets full of new houses on the hill above the dock soon began to mushroom into existence. Many of these early properties had thatched roofs but, once the railway link between the town and Cardiff was established, the supply of good Welsh slate quickly put paid to these semi-rural cottages.

Census returns indicate that in 1841 there were just 96 inhabited houses in Penarth. By 1851 this figure had risen only to 99. Then came the Penarth Harbour and Railway Company and by the time of the 1861 census there were no fewer than 375 inhabited dwellings in the town. The population increased from 466 in 1851 to 1959 ten years later. By 1871 that figure was up yet again, this time to 2652. That represents a percentage increase in the population of 320% for the ten year period between 1851 and 1861, 35% for the next decade – staggering figures by any standards.

In the early years of the town most of the inhabitants came from the county of Glamorgan but as news of the dock development spread, and the insatiable demand for more workmen increased, people began to flock to the new town from all quarters of the country. As early as 1851 they were journeying from Bristol and Somerset in order to establish better lives for themselves in and around the Cardiff/Penarth area. Within twenty years the list of towns and counties where Penarth residents had been born included such far away places as Scotland and Ireland, Pembrokeshire, Yorkshire, London and Cornwall.

By the end of the nineteenth century quiet and empty streets were the hallmark of the town - although the pubs often told a different story.

Despite the fact that new houses had been built to accommodate the workforce there was, inevitably, much over-crowding in the town. The 1861 census shows that the average number of people in each of the town's houses was 5.2. The new houses were quite large, however, and so the over-crowding was not always the problem it might seem. Large families were the order of the day, five or six children for each husband and wife being a fairly common occurrence.

Given the diversity of the population, plus the problems of over-crowding, there is little wonder that the town had something of a reputation for drunkenness and violence in its first few years. The Police Courts were certainly very busy, crimes such as drunkenness and smuggling being quite commonplace. As with any port or dock town, smuggling of tobacco and brandy were the main offences. In one celebrated incident in 1869 sailors from the steamer 'Hartlepool' were apprehended by Customs Officer Mitchell. He thought that their legs looked rather over-sized as they left their ship one evening in March and when their sea boots were forcibly removed it was discovered that they were packed with tobacco.

Poaching was another common crime in these early years and, of course, the standard port offence of sailors failing to return to ship. In 1871, for example, George Andrews of the brig 'Mary Anning,' out of Portsmouth, failed to report for duty. The 'Cardiff Times' of 21st October 1871 reported that he had

The docks brought prosperity as ships from all over the world arrived in Penarth to load their cargoes of coal.

"signed articles - - - as a Cook and Steward, but instead of proceeding on board on the stipulated day, was found in the company of prostitutes."

For his crime Andrews was sent to prison for 14 days of hard labour. There is no doubt that sailors in the Victorian Age lived hard and difficult lives, as did the dock labourers and workmen who serviced their vessels when in port. Public houses were one of the few means of alleviating the hard daily grind. Beer was relatively cheap and, in Penarth, at least, easily accessible. In 1841 there were only two inns or public houses in Penarth but by 1871 this had increased to twelve. These included places like The Merrie Harrier, the Windsor Hotel, the Golden Lion, the Albion, the Pilot and the Clive Arms – all of which are still operating in the town.

Prostitutes regularly plied their wares in Cardiff and Penarth and thieving, pick pocketing and violence were rife, both in the streets and in the pubs. The Cardiff papers of the time – there being, initially at least, no local Penarth paper - are full of stories about seamen being robbed of their wages in public houses and brothels. Yet, amazingly, despite crimes and offences like these, the newcomers – sailors who chose to make the town their home, labourers who came to build the docks and stayed to work them - quickly began to weld themselves into a tightly knit community.

Work had begun on building Penarth Dock in 1859. By that time the Crimean War – as well as the subsequent Indian Mutiny - had already run its course. The Crimean War began in 1853 and British involvement lasted from March 1854 until March 1856, during which time Penarth was only just beginning to develop. There were some Penarth connections with the war, however, as several of the men who came to live in the town had served in the campaign, battling against the ineptitude of their generals and the inadequacies of the War Office as much as the Russian armies that they faced in the field.

Sergeant Major S A Jenkins served throughout the campaign and, interestingly, went on, as a very aged veteran, to recruit young Penarth volunteers during the First World War. John Marshall came from Cornwall and was, for many years, the manager of the Penarth Docks Branch of the Metropolitan Bank. He had been gazetted as an Ensign in 1853 and was due to embark for the Crimea but, probably quite fortunately, illness prevented him joining his regiment. Instead he took up an alternative career and moved to Penarth. He eventually died from bronchitis in November 1901 – had he taken ship for the Crimea his life would probably have been considerably shorter.

Mr C Norman of Cawnpore Road in Cogan was a renowned veteran of the Crimean War – three of his grandsons later went on to serve in the Great War. E Alwyn Benjamin, in his book "Penarth 1841-71," mentions William Sadler (or Saddlier), as being listed on the 1861 census. He was a 32 year old haulier and was supposedly a Crimea veteran who was:-

"hospitalised at Florence Nightingale's hospital at Scutari, but survived to follow a number of civilian occupations. At the time of the 1861 census, he was listed as a publican. It is surmised that his public house was the Clive Arms at Penarth. He later became a shopkeeper and to the present day the business is still in family hands."

When Lance Corporal Donald Boulton won the Military Medal in Normandy in 1944, "The Penarth Times" commented that he came from a military family and that his grandfather was one of the survivors of the Charge of the Light Brigade. Nothing else is known about the man, however. There are probably several others who had Crimean connections but at this distance it is hard to find absolute proof.

The 1881 census returns show that one of the few military men living in the town at the time was James Matthews, a Sergeant in the Royal Artillery. He had been born in Ireland, his wife Philippa in Cornwall. In 1881 they had eight children, two of the daughters having been born at South Hook Fort and Thorne Island Fort in Milford Haven, presumably while their father had been serving with the artillery, defending nearby Pembroke Dockyard.

There was also Amos Jinkins – the name might, possibly, be a miss-print of Jenkins – who, in 1881, was listed as an army pensioner/drill instructor. He was born at St Andrews Major in the Vale of Glamorgan but in 1881 was living with his wife and five children in Ludlow Street, Penarth. Whether Jinkins or Matthews had any experience of the Crimean War is now impossible to say.

One other connection, albeit tenuous, to the Crimean War comes in the shape of Brunel's steamer the 'Great Britain.' Launched from Bristol in 1843, she took soldiers and supplies to the Crimea and to India during the Mutiny of 1857-59. The 'Great Britain' left No 9 Tip, Penarth Dock several years later, her last cruise, on 6th February 1886. She was eventually abandoned in the Falkland Islands where she lay for almost one hundred years – it is a thin and dubious connection but a connection none the less.

In the years between the opening of the docks and the end of the nineteenth century the town was full of sea-faring men. It is understandable as the docks were growing rapidly in these years and sailors would have come flocking to the port, eager for work. While none of them had been born in Penarth they were all in-comers in the period following the town's inception. Captain Thomas Lewis, aged 75 years old, was staying at 64 Maughan Street on census night 1881 but as he was a Pembrokeshire man who was simply visiting the house owner, William Richards, he does not really qualify as a Penarth resident.

The 1881 census for Penarth lists 37 men under the term "Mariners," 17 more under the heading of "Sailors." In addition, a further five young men, all either 15 or 16 years old, are listed as boarding with Mr Sydney B Fox, a Licensed Shipping Agent, at 12 Windsor Road. Clearly they were Apprentices, Sailor Pupils as the census records them, waiting to take ship from the docks. The census also lists eight sailor's wives whose husbands were, presumably, at sea on census night.

An additional 15 people were also listed as "Looking for a ship." These included men like Joseph Culliford, a rigger, and William Jenkins, a ship's fireman. However – and rather surprisingly - this section also included some of the hugely rich ship owners, people like John Corey and Henry Vellacott, who were now beginning to make the town their home. These men lived at the western end of Penarth in places such as Beach Road, clearly keeping themselves quite separate from labourers like Culliford and Jenkins in Glebe and Maughan Streets respectively. They would not be likely to be "Looking for a ship" and that makes their inclusion in the section all the more puzzling.

In the summer months thousands of day trippers flocked to the sea front for a few hours of leisure and pleasure on the beach and pier.

The Coastguard had long had a presence in Penarth, the first set of Coastguard Cottages being built on land overlooking the dock in 1841. However, there was only one lifeboat to cover the whole of the south Wales coast and that was far away at Swansea. It meant that when the docks at Penarth were opened and the amount of shipping in the area greatly increased, the task of saving life after a shipwreck fell solely to the Coastguard. The RNLI finally agreed to provide a lifeboat and a new station was opened in a spot close to the town's Yacht Club. The lifeboat station operated until 1905 when it was closed in favour of a newer one at Barry.

Clearly, then, the influences in the early days of the town were maritime rather than military. Within twenty years things had begun to change and soldiers as well as sailors were beginning to throng the streets of the town. In the 1840s a large mansion house had been built on the headland overlooking the Channel and the docks. When Penarth Head Fort and a coastal battery were created in the immediate vicinity in the 1890s – with a view to protecting Penarth Roads and the docks – the house became the Officers Quarters and was renamed Artillery House.

The people of Penarth did not relish the idea of a fort in their midst. British soldiers had never had an enviable reputation with the public, most people being unable to forget the words of the Duke of Wellington when looking at his troops on the eve of Waterloo – "I don't know what they do to the French, but they terrify me!" Also the cliffs below the proposed fort on Penarth Head were brittle and fragile and there was a very real possibility of the explosions and shock waves from the guns setting off serious cliff falls.

In a wonderfully ironic and satirical leader article, the editor of "The Penarth Observer" seemed to catch the mood of the moment when he wrote, on 13th May 1892:-

"Many local gentlemen who are entitled to write Colonel, Major, Captain etc before their names have written in that we are - - - defenceless should an enemy send an ironclad up Channel to attack us. I hear a subscription is about to be started to defray the cost of mounting a Gatling Gun and two pea shooters on the tower of the church; this should frighten 'the darned Mounseer.'"

Protests and complaints were of little use, the military would come. With nearby Lavernock also in use as a base for summer camps Penarth was soon full of "the brutal and licentious soldiery." Careful study of the local papers in the town over the first two decades of the twentieth century, reveal that, in many respects, the people of Penarth were not far wrong in their fears of the soldiers behaviour – but more of this later.

By 1865, at almost all states of the tide, dozens of square rigged sailing ships were to be found lying in close proximity to each other in the Channel off Penarth and Cardiff, waiting to come into port and load up with coal. In such a crowded environment it was inevitable that accidents should occur. Seafaring was a difficult and dangerous occupation, Board of Trade figures showing that in 1861 alone 4000 sailors died. That statistic means that one in every 56 of the men who went to sea met an untimely death. In the next four decades, to the end of the nineteenth century, nothing changed very much. The "Cardiff Times" of 8th July 1871 records just one example:-

"Yesterday a fatal accident happened on the brig 'Coldstream' of Ipswich, then lying in Penarth Roads. A seaman named William Taylor, aged 20, was aloft loosening the foresail when he slipped and fell from the foreyard onto the deck."

Taylor was rushed to the 'Hamadryad' hospital ship in Cardiff Docks but, unfortunately, he died later that evening.

Fire was a constant hazard on wooden ships and there are several recorded instances of ships in Penarth being severely damaged in this way. Fire was discovered on board the barque 'Giulietta' in March 1871 – she was towed out of the shipping lanes in Penarth Roads but sank on the eastern mud flats of the bay. Similarly, the 'Psyche' caught fire in December of the same year. Despite the exertions of the Cardiff Fire Brigade, the 'Psyche' sank in thirty foot of water in Penarth Dock. The incident is interesting because Cardiff Fire Brigade was called, there being no fire engine in Penarth Dock, and by the time the brigade arrived the fire had taken hold. The ship was doomed.

Health and Safety was not really an issue in these years. There was a job to be done and if it involved a degree of risk then that was simply the way of the world. There are many instances of workmen being killed in the docks, falling from gantries or being crushed by loose cargoes. Some of the stories are tragic in the extreme. The same Joseph Culliford who had been listed as "Looking for a ship" in the 1881 census was killed when he fell into the dock on 22nd September 1893 – as if the family had not suffered enough, his son Ted was later shot through the heart and killed by a sniper during the Great War.

The docks might well have offered secure employment to hundreds of in-coming workers but that did not mean they would tolerate bad conditions. In 1863 there was a strike when 214 masons and 84 gantry-men withdrew their labour as a result of the company trying to reduce their wages by three pence a day when wages were over 4 shillings and 6 pence, two pence per day when they were below. It was just one of several examples of men "downing tools" but, despite such incidents, by 1883 Penarth Docks were already highly successful, exporting 2,274,003 tons of coal each year.

The years leading up to the end of the nineteenth century saw rapid development of the town's streets, roadways and public buildings. It was in this brief but hugely influential period that most of the building blocks that now go to make up modern Penarth were first established. It was an important time in the history of the town.

However, there seems to have been something of a split personality as far as the town's development and direction were concerned in these years. The industrial sprawl of the docks had spawned the town in the first place and there is no doubt that they brought considerable wealth to the community. Yet it was as a holiday resort that the town's founding fathers really wanted the place to operate.

The Esplanade was built between 1883 and 1884, a huge and elegant walkway that symbolised the town's desire to achieve a position of supremacy in Welsh seaside towns. The beach had always been a draw for the people of nearby Cardiff, most of them travelling to Penarth by ferry boats like the 'Kate,' 'Iona' and 'La Belle Marie' and landing across the shingle. Some better means of enabling people to enjoy the delights of the sea front and town was clearly

Windsor Road, the town's main thoroughfare, in the days before the arrival of the motor car.

needed. After much debate and procrastination, a pier was built and opened in 1895. With its elegant gardens and parks, the Esplanade Hotel, its swimming pools and Yacht Club, Penarth now seemed ready to claim the number one spot. A small hiccup, however, was about to occur.

"The Penarth Observer" for Saturday 7th October 1899 brought more than a few moments of disquiet to the residents of the town:-

"The news to hand is ominous, the Boers armed for battle have occupied Laing's Neck in menacing array, and the might of Britain is being massed, regardless of cost, against them."

Britain, in 1899, was at the height of its Imperial power and nobody was in the mood to placate the Boer farmers in South Africa. When they tried to reject British control, war was inevitable and Penarth, like the rest of the country, was quickly swept up by the war fervour.

TURNER GALLERY, PENARTH

Penarth at the time of the Boer War - Stanwell Road & the Turner Gallery.

Chapter Two – It's War At Last

The Boer War broke out in October 1899. Actually, this conflict should be more accurately termed the second Boer War, the first war between Britain and the Boers having been little more than a skirmish fought between the years 1880 and 1881. This small colonial scrap had been won by the Boers after a famous victory at Majuba Hill and it had given the Boer Republics of Transvaal and Orange Free State a degree of independence from the British Empire. However, when gold was discovered in the Transvaal in 1886 it was clear that further conflict in South Africa would not be long in coming.

Fuelled by complaints about the mistreatment of immigrant gold diggers – or 'uitlanders' as they were known – and by stories about the Jameson Raid, presented to the public as a brave attempt to rescue British women and children from the tyrannical Boers, there was a massive pro-war mood in the country. And the people of Penarth, like the rest of Britain, were eager to see their army put an end to what they perceived as the insults of Paul Kruger, President of the Transvaal.

"The Penarth Observer" for Saturday 14th October 1899 left readers in no doubt about its feelings and stance:-

"War at last! There can be no question of it; for it is inconceivable that England should bow to the knee to Kruger, to yield meek compliance with his insulting demands to withdraw troops from the borders of Transvaal, to leave Natal practically defenceless and to send home the reinforcements that are already on the seas."

For weeks the pages of the paper had been full of only one topic, the situation in South Africa. Not since the English Civil War in the seventeenth century had members of the general public been called upon to fight in war. Battles had been contested by professional armies, not by the ordinary man in the street. War was seen only at a distance, even the carnage of the Crimean War being, for most people, little more than an excuse for mild recriminations and a shaking of heads over the breakfast newspapers. Now, however, such was the fervour of patriotic sentiment unleashed by the press that men rushed to join the various Yeomanry Regiments and to get out to South Africa to do their bit in giving Kruger and the Boers a bloody nose!

For the young men of Penarth there were really only two choices, the Glamorgan Yeomanry or the Glamorgan Militia Artillery. Of these the former undoubtedly had the most glamour. Dozens of adventurous youths from the town promptly enlisted – and they would be needed.

Yeomanry Volunteers at firing practise.

Before the war was over 450,000 men were serving in South Africa and, of these, over 200,000 were volunteers, from right across Britain, who had enlisted in a burst of patriotic pride within a few months of war being declared. The average death toll during the war was ten men a day and more than a few of these were to come from Penarth.

For almost the first time a Colonial war had seized the public imagination and "The Penarth Observer" for Saturday 4th November 1899 was quick to decry the efforts of the Boers, even though all of the early British advances had been bloodily repulsed. Indeed, with Boer forces besieging towns like Ladysmith and Mafeking it appeared, at first, as if the British Empire was heading for inglorious defeat. For "The Penarth Observer" sarcasm was clearly the best sanctuary:-

The Yeomanry cavalry units quickly became the most popular choice for young men eager to get out to South Africa to "do their bit."

"On the 17th of October the Boers bombarded Mafeking for four hours and killed a dog. On the 23rd they began another bombardment at a range of two miles and a half but did little damage."

On Saturday 16th December the renowned composer Joseph Parry, himself a Penarth resident, gave a concert at the Drill Hall in Woodlands Place in order to raise money towards a relief fund for the families of soldiers and sailors in Penarth. The concert was, apparently, superb and a total of £20 was raised for the fund.

The soldiers themselves, however, men who were being gathered together at Penarth before shipping out to South Africa, were not always easy to accept into such a small community – "The Penarth Observer" again:-

"We hear very bad reports of the behaviour of the Glamorgan Militia Artillery, who have been stationed at Lavernock - - - it appears that a number of them returned to the camp in a riotous drunken condition and that on passing through the lower parts of Westbourne Road and Plymouth Road, they wilfully destroyed a large number of trees there planted."

When Ladysmith was finally relieved early in 1900 there was immediate and unrestrained rejoicing in the town. Flags miraculously appeared on most of the houses, church bells were rung and guns from the fort at Lavernock were fired. Solomon Andrews, the local entrepreneur, gave the town the use of his hall, free of charge, and the District Council organised a public meeting with the aim of allowing people "to let off steam."

At the meeting there was much shouting and stamping of feet, loud cat calls and rowdy behaviour. Congratulatory speeches were given by various local dignitaries, along with songs and recitations. All of this was due to have been followed by music from a band but, in the end,

Off to the war – a late Victorian print showing soldiers embarking on a troop ship.

the musicians did not turn up and the gathering had to content itself with a parade or procession around the streets of the town, making as much noise as was humanly possible.

Apart from celebrations of events like the lifting of the Ladysmith siege, the regular routine of life in Penarth continued much as normal. In late December 1899 there had been a diphtheria scare in the town, the outbreak causing Richard Nell, the Medical Officer of Health, to reassure people that

"there is, at present, only one house in the district affected by diphtheria."

"The Penarth Observer" for 17th February 1900 led with a story about a dishonest Penarth shop keeper:-

"At the Police Court - - - Wm Thomas, grocer, Glebe Street, was charged with selling margarine without being labelled - - - Inspector Williams said that he visited the defendant's shop and found margarine stacked in three heaps on the counter. He asked for three quarters of a pound of butter and was supplied. The sample was afterwards found to be margarine."

Unfortunately, this was Mr Thomas' second appearance before the court and he was fined forty shillings – or one months' hard labour.

Early in May 1900 over 200 workers engaged on extending the docks left their site and poured onto the waiting Cardiff train. They were shouting and laughing and many of the passengers felt sure that Mafeking had finally been relieved. In fact, the men had just gone on strike after having their dinner break reduced to just half an hour.

Mafeking was still under siege – despite many rumours to the contrary - and, for Penarth as well as the rest of Britain, the toll of death and injury was beginning to mount. The town's first recorded casualty was reported in "The Penarth Observer" on 21st April 1900:-

"A letter from Mr S Rooney of the Glamorgan County Yeomanry, from Cape Town, records the death of his comrade, Mr E Morton Hadley, from pneumonia. Both were in hospital at Cape Town but Mr Rooney alone recovered."

Hadley was a Penarth resident where he was a popular and well respected member of the community. Having joined the Yeomanry at the start of the war he had been entertained by his many friends at the Alexandra Hotel in Cardiff before setting off for Newport, ready to take ship to South Africa.

The war against the Boers soon proved far tougher than anyone ever imagined.

The siege of Mafeking was finally lifted at the end of May 1900 and the event, just like the relief of Ladysmith, caused unbridled celebrations in Penarth. Once again, there were parades and speeches and a huge bonfire was quickly built and lit on the headland above the docks, close to the Penarth Head fort.

By now, dozens of Penarth men were serving in South Africa. Among them were Edward Albert Savage, F Taylor, Arthur Howell and E J Wadley. Interestingly, Wadley went on to serve in the Great War where he was mentioned in despatches. Taylor was wounded during the Boer War and was also mentioned in despatches. Like Wadley, he went on to enlist again during the Great War but, because of his age, he was only allowed to serve at home and Ireland.

Mr S Reed, of the 1st Devon's, was another Penarth man, a regular soldier who won two South African campaign medals and went on to serve for twenty years in the army. He was later commissioned as a Second Lieutenant during the Great War but was shot and killed while mending the wire in front of the British trenches a few weeks after joining his Regiment.

"The Penarth Observer" printed a letter from Arthur Howell, former Registrar of Births and Deaths for the town, on Saturday 10th November 1900. Serving with the Glamorgan Yeomanry, the young man commented that he had been

"for the last three weeks in chase of De Wet but had not yet been able to come up with him because the Boers will not stand."

He then went on to talk about how much he looked forward to coming home to Penarth, not least because he might then have something good to eat!

Barely a month later, the same paper announced the death of Lt Harold C Ingram who had lived with his parents in Penarth for many years. Ingram had joined Roberts' Light Horse in January 1899 and was present at the relief of Kimberley under Sir John French. He had been hit in the shoulder by a bullet from a Boer rifleman and was invalided home to Penarth to recover. Despite being told that he was now too old to re-enlist, Ingram obtained a post with the Civil Department and sailed, once again, for South Africa. Once out there he managed to get himself an interview with Roberts and was commissioned, again, into Roberts' Horse. His death was as a result of concussion to the brain, having been thrown from his horse before going into action.

In January 1901 Queen Victoria died, the event being greeted with sombre acceptance in Penarth. As the black-bordered announcement in "The Penarth Observer" said:-

"Victoria the Great lies at rest by the side of Albert the Good."

'Goodbye Dolly, I Must Leave You' soon became one of the most popular soldier's songs of the war – this Victorian print captures the mood of soldiers leaving for South Africa. You can almost hear the song echoing down the station platform.

Death seemed ever-present to the people of Penarth that year. In June a circus elephant, said to be one of those brought by the Prince of Wales from India, collapsed and died while making its way into the town. All of the other circus animals apparently stood and stared at their fallen comrade as they went past and one of the lions even reared up onto his back legs and kept his eyes fixed on the prostrate elephant for several minutes as his cage rattled down the street.

In December "The Penarth Observer" was commenting:-

"On Thursday, during the dinner hour, one of the horses attached to Messrs Andrews and Sons buses fell down in a dying state, after climbing the hill just abreast of the Police Station. As there was no hope of its living, one of the police constables put an end to its existence by shooting. Naturally the passengers were somewhat upset by the disagreeable circumstances."

The Penarth Police Court was also very busy in 1901. On 1st June Captain William Jones of the steamer 'Dunraven' was charged with assaulting the ship's cook, a man called Moses Thomas:-

"The complainant's case was that the Captain had occasion to complain of the quality of the soup provided for dinner, and struck him repeatedly, giving him a black eye. While the Captain was striking him, one of the officers held him. The Captain's defence was that the complainant refused to go out of the cabin when requested to do so."

Amazingly, the case was dismissed. On 12th August Charles Linser was convicted of creating a disturbance and with assaulting PC Fahy. Linser was apparently walking and dancing along Windsor Road shouting "We are going to stop the war!" When asked to desist he refused and kicked the policeman several times in the leg. This time there was no leniency from the Bench and Linser was duly fined.

That same week Catherine Lewis, a widow from Windsor Road, was charged with threatening Elizabeth Norman. Seemingly there had been a dispute between the two women after Lewis bought a carriage from Norman for £10. The carriage broke apart in Windsor Road, the pony running away with the two front wheels – to the undoubted amusement of the local youths. Lewis was bound over for £5 to keep the peace for the next six months.

Also that August, John Vickery, the landlord of the Cefn Mably Inn, was charged with selling watered down gin. The analyst certified that the sample he had been given was no less than 46% under proof.

Meanwhile the war in South Africa ground remorselessly on. On August 20th the War Office despatched a telegram to Mrs Hole of 1 Cornerswell Road –

"Regret to inform you your son 31324 W Hole, Imperial Yeomanry, severely wounded, 16th August. No further details."

Trooper Hole was just one in a long line of Penarth injured. By now the war seemed to have been dragging on for a very long time. The Boers, although clearly in retreat, were refusing to lie down and accept defeat and a mood of disquiet seemed to have infected much of Britain. At the Penarth Police Court in March 1902 Percy Bernard, a young soldier from Cogan, was charged with being drunk and disorderly. Bernard threw himself on the mercy of the court, stating that he was going to the front on active service and was leaving on Good Friday. The magistrate wished him good luck and discharged him with a caution.

On 26th April 1902 "The Penarth Observer" reported that:-

"the family of Mr J Carey Thomas has sustained a very painful bereavement in the death of his second son, C Oswald Thomas, at the front, on the 20th inst. He went to South Africa as a member of the Glamorgan Yeomanry, subsequently joining the Wiltshire Yeomanry. It is particularly painful to state that he had received orders to return home and would have started in a few days time, but he fell in the recent fighting at Oliviers Farm. His age was but 24."

C Oswald Thomas was the last Penarth casualty of the Boer War. On Sunday 1st June 1902 the town heard the news that peace had been declared. The next night, Monday 2nd June, a Thanksgiving Service was held at Christ Church, led by Rev J G Jones. For most of the people in Penarth, however, celebrations were somewhat more lively. As "The Penarth |Observer" of the following week commented:-

"Well meant, as an evidence of the exuberant joy of the populace, it degenerated into sheer masquerading and tomfoolery, or 'mafficking' as it is called."

There was not much evidence of excessive drinking in the town but there was a great deal of rowdy behaviour as a make-shift procession wound its way around the streets:-

"Mr Thomas, chairman of the Council, addressed a few words to the excited throng, amid such noises that it was with difficulty that he could make himself heard. His words were well chosen – 'Thank you one and all for so ably assisting in this demonstration. I hope you will remember that henceforward we are fellow citizens of the Boers.'"

In due course the men came home from the war, bringing with them their memories and experiences. The name Spion Kop, after a South African hill, soon became a common term for one of the huge spoil heaps at the Billybanks. Situated close to The Royal Hotel on the north edge of Penarth Ridge, the Billybanks area once held at least five small quarries. The spoil heaps for the quarries became known as "mountains" or "banks" to the people of Penarth, hence the term Billybanks.

The war against the Boers might have been over but the remorseless campaign by the Penarth authorities against unseemly behaviour continued. The town pier and beach were to prove the major battleground. For too long people had been bathing naked on the beach and "The Penarth Observer" was soon commenting on what it called "offences against decency" –

"Five boys were summoned for bathing without proper dress - - - Four of them made no defence and were fined 1s each. The fifth, Warren Thomas, son of Mr Carey Thomas, it appears, was insolent to the officer and had - - - two witnesses to appear on his behalf. They alleged that he had been properly attired but was drying himself when accosted."

Soldiers might be dying in the war against the Boers but back home in Penarth life went on much as before with dozens of visitors arriving each year to walk on the pier and sit on the beach.

Thomas was found guilty and also fined one shilling. Interestingly, Carey Thomas was also the father of the town's last casualty in the recent war but no allowances seem to have been made.

The town continued to grow, census returns for 1891 showing that the population then had been 12,424 – as the century drew to a close everyone knew that figure had only become larger. And the docks, too, continued to be successful. Statements of trade for the year 1902 show that 2347 steam vessels had cleared the docks during the preceding year as well as 913 sailing ships, giving a total number of 3290 ships passing through the port. A total of 3,469,159 tons of product had been exported, 3,467,538 tons of that being coal and coke. Imports amounted to 123,950 tons, most of that being either gas coal or general merchandise.

As the nineteenth century drew to a close Penarth, as a town, had been in existence for nearly forty years and many of its older citizens were, quite naturally, beginning to die off. A plaque in St Augustine's Church records the life and achievements of just one of them:-

"In memory of Commander Walter Murray Pengelly (of Her Majesty's Late Indian Navy), for twenty years Dockmaster at Penarth who died December 29th 1897. He was for many years Honorary Secretary of the Penarth Branch of the Missions to Seamen and by his influence the church and Institute connected to that Mission were erected in 1878 at Penarth Dock. He was also Honorary Secretary from 1875 to 1897 of the Penarth Branch of the Royal National Lifeboat Institution. He was a thorough Christian and a true friend of the sailor and Churchwarden of this church from 1878 to 1880."

In August 1902 a curious and amazing accident took place on Penarth Head. Playing with his friends, five year old Alfred White missed his footing and fell headlong to the beach below. It was a drop of over 100 foot but, although knocked unconscious by the fall, the boy sustained no serious injury and he soon recovered.

Penarth Pier continued to be a big draw in the first decade of the twentieth century. In 1907 a wooden pavilion had been built on the seaward end of the pier and here managers like Oscar Mills and Alfred Newton brought countless acts to entertain visitors and residents alike. The Royal Court Entertainers, Montague's Mountebanks, The Court Jesters and the Mad Hatters, Penarth Pier Bijou Pavilion saw them all.

The paddle steamers of the White Funnel Fleet and the Barry Railway Company called, regularly, at the pier. For a few shillings people could take a cruise across the Channel to places like Weston-super-Mare or Ilfracombe on board the 'Waverly,' 'Cambria' and 'Ravenswood.' If they couldn't afford the fare there was always the pier to walk on or ices and cups of tea to be had from Salter's Pier Café.

In the sunlit world of Edwardian Britain it sometimes seemed as if prosperity and access to the good things in life were the right of everyone. There were the occasional hitches, of course, but when they came, people tended to look for the good and discount the bad. So when, in 1912, the news filtered through that Captain Scott and his party had died attempting to reach the South Pole it was the heroism of the explorer that they applauded. Freezing to death with Wilson and Bowers, his last two companions, in a tent in the wastes of Antarctica - but somehow still summoning the courage and fortitude to write his famous last message to the British populace – that was the image people chose to remember. The poor planning and the foolhardy, stiff upper lip attitudes that permeated the whole expedition were quickly and easily overlooked. Scott and his ship 'Terra Nova' had appeared off Penarth in June 1910, en route for Antarctica, and so the people of the town had a particular fondness for the man and his mission.

Scott's 'Terra Nova' off Penarth Head in 1910.

The 'Titanic' disaster of 1912 stunned the world, almost 1500 passengers and crew drowning when the giant liner struck an iceberg in the Atlantic. Like many communities in Britain, Penarth had its 'Titanic' connections, young James Reed from the town being one of the fatalities. He is commemorated on a plaque in Trinity Church. The Plaque reads:-

"In memory of James Reed, aged 18 years, who was drowned in the RMS Titanic disaster, April 15th 1912. Erected by the members of his Sunday School class."

The plaque in Trinity Church commemorating the death of James Reed in the 'Titanic' disaster – just before he sailed the young man wrote to his mother asking for his pen knife to be forwarded to him. He never received it.

Little more is known about Reed. However, there is another rarely mentioned 'Titanic' connection with the town. One of the first admissions to the Gibbs Home in the early 1920s was Edwin Meak. His placement was partially funded by the Titanic Relief Fund as his mother had been one of the victims when the liner sank. She had taken a steerage ticket with a view to starting a new life in America.

The disaster touched everyone in Britain and the people of Penarth were as keen to help as anyone. A garden party was held in Windsor Gardens in aid of the relief fund in May 1912 when even heavy rain did not prevent a large sum of money being raised. "The Penarth Times" for 25th April 1912 announced that

"A sacred play, entitled 'St Albn,' will be performed at St Augustine's Church Institute on Monday and Tuesday next - - - by the Penarth Amateur Dramatic Society. The proceeds were originally intended for the Institute funds but the members of the above society have unanimously decided to divide the net proceeds equally between the Titanic Disaster and the Institute funds."

By 1913 the new-fangled "moving pictures" had well and truly arrived in Penarth. The Windsor Kinema was advertising "Heroes One and All," a magnificent two-part drama with "some thrilling fire scenes." It was to be followed by 'From the Depths of the Sea' which prided itself as being:-

"a subject of breathless interest with many hair-breath escapes on and off railway trains, a fight in a motor car and escape on the sails of a windmill. And finally, a splendidly realistic underwater scene where the hero recovers precious papers from the bottom of the sea."

As 1914 dawned the people of Penarth had little or no idea that the world was about to change forever. Indeed, the most important announcement in "The Penarth Times" for 1st January was that Penarth rugby team had lost their ground record. In what might later be regarded as a prophetic statement, the paper said:-

"throughout the game it was the forwards who bore the brunt of the battle."

The comparison to the thousands of foot soldiers who would soon be floundering through fields of mud is, perhaps, a little too painful to consider for long.

BUCKINGHAM PALACE.

I join with my grateful people
in sending you this memorial
of a brave life given for others
in the Great War.

George R.I.

Chapter Three – The Great War

There are approximately 36,000 memorials in Britain to the men who died in the First World War, the Great War as the soldiers invariably called it. These memorials often began with small street shrines erected by the people of the area but such was the extent of the carnage caused by the conflict that local authorities eventually had no choice other than to provide some form of official commemoration.

Penarth has a large number and wide range of memorials to the men of the town who fell in the Great War. Quite apart from the official War Memorial in Alexandra Park, there are plaques and tablets in churches, in public and private buildings - and in the lounge of Glamorganshire Golf Club. Other memorials include a sports grandstand and even a school!

As 1914 dawned, however, the people of Penarth had no idea of what was awaiting them. "The Penarth Times" announced the coming of the New Year in hopeful but, perhaps, prophetic style:-

"A delightful star-lit night heralded the incoming of the New Year, and hundreds traversing our streets exchanged the old greeting 'A Happy New Year' - - - We cannot penetrate into the future. The most we can do is hope."

Austria and Serbia went to war that summer and the steady progression of ultimatums and treaty obligations saw more and more European nations gradually joining the conflict. To many it seemed only a matter of time before Britain joined in and, to begin with, a degree of mild panic appeared to descend on Penarth. The Glamorgan Royal Engineers left the town, en route to Pembroke Dock and duties abroad, and at the end of July a new detachment of troops took possession of Penarth Head Fort. Armed police were on duty, day and night, at the docks and, more worryingly for the householders of the town, the price of bread went up by one penny per loaf. As the crisis deepened there were further increases in the price of bacon, tea, sugar, tinned goods and rice.

Britain formally entered the war on 4th August, in an attempt to protect the neutrality of tiny Belgium. The immediate response to the war from within the town was not enthusiastic. At Stanwell Road Baptist Chapel the Rev Gwilym O Griffiths preached a sermon protesting against Britain's involvement in a war that should, he felt, be concerning only Russia, France and Germany. A resolution was passed deploring the situation and urging Sir Edward Grey, the Foreign Secretary, not to relax his peace efforts for one second.

Local trade was severely affected during the first few days of the war. Grocery shops in particular soon found that their shelves were almost empty due to an unprecedented "laying in" of supplies by those who had money to spend. Shop assistants were starting work early in the morning and then staying on late into the evening to cope with demand. In other trades, however, the effect of being at war worked the other way. Summer visitors began to leave the town in their droves, leaving hotels and guest houses empty, while many employers like the railway companies and the Post Office immediately cancelled their workers leave and called them back to duty.

From the day war was declared all ships entering Penarth were boarded outside the docks, their captains questioned and the vessels searched. Special tugs had been engaged for this duty and officers appointed specifically for the task.

From 13th August "The Penarth Times" introduced a "War News in Brief" column to the paper and at the end of the month the National Union of Women's Suffrage Society – the Suffragettes - announced that it had suspended its political activities for the time being. The Penarth Committee of the Suffragettes had already approached the District Council, offering to help with "visiting and distributing clothes and provisions."

On 27th August "The Penarth Times" was commenting on what had suddenly become a serious problem for local businesses:-

"Owing to the Admiralty commandeering so many horses from Penarth, several local firms are considering the purchase of motor delivery vans."

It is an interesting development - pragmatism at its best or a gradual realisation that the twentieth century had well and truly dawned?

Recruiting for the forces quickly gathered pace within the town, young men being lured to the colours by dreams of glory and by posters of Lord Kitchener's sombre face declaring that their "King and Country" needed them. By the end of August, in a period of just three weeks, over 400 Penarth men had joined the army and, occasionally, the navy, all eager to "do their bit" before the great adventure finished without them. There was a strong belief, fuelled by a strident and increasingly warlike press, that the war would be over by Christmas – the German Kaiser, interestingly, thought the same, declaring that his troops would be home "before the leaves fall from the trees."

Yet no matter how many men enlisted, more were always needed and in an article headlined "Clear out the Cowards!" "The Penarth Times" left readers in no doubt about where it stood on the issue of enlistment:-

Sketches
of Tommy's life
In Training. — N° 1

" That seems to mean me all right "

When the Great War broke out in 1914 there was an urgent need for volunteers – as this postcard of the time shows.

"a few days ago Belgium was smiling and happy. Now, with her sons slaughtered and her daughters subjected to unspeakable atrocities, everywhere is ruins and misery – and simply because Belgium objected to a strange army passing through her territory. If Germany metes out such treatment to Belgium, what mercy can Britain expect? Yet our young men go about in their tennis rig-outs or parade on the Esplanade, smirking at girls. Is it fair that they should go about so callously whilst those who took up arms with our promised support, lie cold and stiff?"

The article went on to urge the girls of Penarth to give "the laggards" their marching orders, to shame them into understanding where their duty lay.

The real nature of war soon revealed itself to the people of Penarth, however. In early September the town learned of the death in action, during the retreat from Mons, of the Hon Archer Windsor-Clive, the second son of the Earl of Plymouth and a man with considerable Penarth connections.

Another early casualty was Albert (Bertie) Bartlett of Dock Street who was also killed during the Battle of Mons, on 23rd August, the first of three brothers to die during the war. He was 29 years old.

Lt R Harrison of Kymin Terrace was luckier. He was on board the 'Cressey,' sunk by the torpedoes of U9 on 22nd September, along with the 'Hogue' and 'Aboukir.' The 'Aboukir' was hit first and the other cruisers stopped to pick up survivors, their captains not understanding that a new and brutal type of warfare had arrived. Out of 2000 men on board the three ships over 1400 perished. Lt Harrison was in the water for one and a half hours before being picked up by a trawler.

That same month the firing of the guns from Penarth Fort caused some alarm for the residents of the town. Many believed that the Germans had landed but, in reality, the artillery men were engaging in a little target practise, firing at the wreck of the SS 'Acolus' which had lain on the rocks close to Flat Holm for the past two years. Three shots were fired, two of them hitting the wreck and holing it but otherwise causing little or no damage.

● 12159   ST. AUGUSTINE'S CHURCH, PENARTH.

As casualty lists mounted, St Augustine's Church set up a 'Roll of Honour' to commemorate the men who had lost their lives in the war.

An article in "The Penarth Times" early in September declared that the town pubs had been served with an early closing notice and that, as a consequence, there had been a great reduction in the ribaldry that had been caused by soldiers stationed in the town. It brought a furious response from Captain A P Thomas, who commanded the Royal Garrison Artillery at the fort. Refuting the implications about his men he declared that

"Firstly, no men from this Battery are ever out - - - after 7.30 pm. Secondly, 60 per cent are total abstainers."

It seems an amazing claim but, at the time – and remembering the mood of patriotic jingoism in the country – his words seem to have been accepted as absolute fact. That jingoism was certainly causing problems for some of the people in the town. A letter from Jules Guldentops of Lord Street shows how misplaced patriotism could cause considerable pain and unhappiness:-

"I have been taken for a German many times and I am very sorry to see the public is under a misapprehension as to my nationality. I was born in Mons, Belgium. I came to Cardiff twenty seven years ago. My wife is a native of Wales. After being so many years in Great Britain, with the British public, I call myself a British patriot."

The real tragedy behind the issue is the fact that Mr Guldentops felt he had to write the letter in the first place! Yet prejudice, bigotry and thinly-disguised bullying were rife in the town at this time. A letter to "The Penarth Times" that November, signed by someone calling himself "Fairplay" serves as an example:-

"Some German aliens are still in our midst. Some are educated and some are not but this writer would like to know why some are interned and some are not. The highly educated alien is of more danger to the public than the less educated."

While the war in France proceeded apace there were several incidents of note back home in Penarth. One early morning a sentry on duty between St Augustine's Church and the Penarth Fort was actually fired on by somebody hiding himself in the undergrowth. The sentry returned fire with a couple of shots but the assailant managed to escape – a prank, perhaps, but a dangerous one, not to say foolhardy.

The fear of spies caused a furore in the town one summer day. A strange man was spotted walking along Windsor Road, asking passers-by about the deployment of troops in the area. Mr A I Beer followed and then chased the man as far as Riverside but lost him in the warren of streets. Early in 1915 there was another "spy scare" when a man was arrested at the docks but it soon transpired that the supposed German agent was actually a Swede who had been visiting the port for the past twenty years. On 10th December a man was seen prowling near the power station in the docks. When he was challenged the prowler fired twice and then made good his escape. Such stories probably say more about the over-fertile imagination of the sentries, on edge in the darkness, than they do about the realities of fifth columnists or spies.

As the first year of war drew to a close, there were, increasingly, stories in the local papers about soldiers serving in France and, more and more often, notices announcing the deaths of Penarth men. The death of Major Charles Christie was recorded that October and in November the news was received that Stoker Frederick Morris from Cogan had been killed on board HMS 'Monmouth'. The 'Monmouth' had been sunk, along with the 'Good Hope' at the Battle of Coronel – a defeat later avenged at the Battle of the Falkland Islands, where Penarth sailor H Allen took part as a member of the crew of HMS 'Canopus.' In December came the news that Private George Wright, wounded at Ypres, had died while Lt Paterson, the son-in-law of Mr Carey Thomas – who had already lost a son in the Boer War – had been taken prisoner.

Campbell's steamers had suspended their cruises when war broke out, only the old 'Waverley' being retained to run a makeshift service between the Welsh coast and Weston.

The Christmas truce of 1914 has been described many times but Private Frank Pope, of Cogan Hall - himself later to become a casualty of the war - was in the trenches over that period. He wrote to his family about the moment and, rather more fully, about the subsequent New Year celebrations:-

Private Percy Hoult, Lance Corporal Burge and Second Lt Farquahar-Thompson. They were all men who had happily marched off to war in 1914 – sadly, the reality of the situation was now beginning to hit home.

Towards the end of 1915 Penarth saw its first deserter when George Henry Cox, a private in the RGA, appeared before the Police Court. He was handed over to a military escort who were waiting, ready, in the court. That same month "The Penarth Times" published a story that seemed to sum up the changing times:-

"On Sunday evening a young woman passed down Glebe Street and through Windsor Road complacently and brazenly smoking a cigar with all the ease and frankness of a veteran of the weed. In Windsor Road a number of boys looked like making a demonstration and following the woman but she was allowed to proceed unmolested."

At this distance the shock of such an event on the staid and conservative streets of Penarth can only be imagined!

As 1916 dawned the end of the war seemed no closer. Yet there was still a desire to see things through to the end. Private J Glaves from Glebe Street summed it up in a poem he wrote that year, part of which is reproduced here:-

"We've stuck it now for twenty months
And we'll stick it twenty more,
And we'll stick it twenty after that
Till we get to Berlin's door."

There was an outbreak of smallpox in Penarth that spring but as the cases were all restricted to just one family in Cogan it did not cause too much of a problem to the authorities. Visitors to the town in 1916 were limited as the pier had been requisitioned by the army and most of the Campbell steamers were now serving as minesweepers with the navy. Two of them, 'Brighton Queen' and 'Lady Ismay,' had already been lost in action and only the old 'Waverley' and 'Glen Rosa' were operating a limited service between Cardiff and Weston.

Interestingly, Corporal Scarrett of Dock Street returned to Penarth in February 1916, having been posted missing some eleven months previously. He had spent the time in hiding behind enemy lines, waiting for his chance to escape. The famous Nurse Edith Cavell helped him, giving him 45 francs to enable him to get over the frontier. Scarrett was the last British soldier she was able to help as she was arrested, tried and shot by the Germans shortly afterwards. Promoted to Sergeant, Scarrett had soon been re-mustered and sent back to France where, in August, he was severely wounded by shrapnel.

MEN OF PENARTH!

YOU who are physically unfit for the Regular Army,

OR over the enlistable age,

OR engaged on Government work and cannot be enlisted

You have YOUR opportunity !

JOIN THE

Volunteer Training Corps

First Class Drill and Musketry Instruction.
Good Indoor Range for Evening practice.
Use of Drill Hall two nights a week.
Uniform may be paid for in instalments.

Come along to the Drill Hall on Monday or Thursday after 7-30.

NO SHIRKERS NEED APPLY.

A fore-runner of the Home Guard, this advert asked for men to join the Penarth Volunteer Training Corps to help defend the British homeland.

In June 1916 the great naval Battle of Jutland took place and several Penarth men were present. W T Cook was saved when his ship, the cruiser 'Warrior,' was sunk but Engine Room Artificer W T Watkins, from Dock Road, died when the battle cruiser 'Indefatigable' blew up in the early stages of the battle. Royal Marine gunner William George Burge and Ordinary Seaman Chas Roberts also died during the battle when the battle cruiser 'Queen Mary' came under the guns of the German battleships and was blown apart. Stoker Chris Shepherd on board Beatty's flagship 'Lion' was another Penarth man who came through the encounter unscathed.

Another navy man, Sub Lt Alex Daniels from Windsor Terrace was awarded the DSC that year. He was serving on board the 'Albion,' a White Funnel paddle steamer that Penarth people were more used to seeing moored to their pier but had now been commandeered by the Admiralty for mine sweeping duties.

One of the many fascinating Penarth residents at this time was Miss Ann Jones Pearce. Well remembered in the town as a former scholar of Stanwell Road Sunday School, she left Penarth shortly after the start of the war to take charge of a Red Cross Unit in Serbia.

There are no records dealing with how Miss Pearce coped with what was undoubtedly a major culture shock. Penarth, then, was a bastion of middle class, non-conformist values. Serbia, on the other hand, was a backward, almost medieval country where serfdom was rife and the regime totalitarian. What is clear is that Ann Pearce was a formidable woman – she survived the experience.

After the war Miss Pearce settled in London where she became the proprietor of a Nursing Home in Wanstead. Her father, incidentally, was a master stone craftsman who came to Penarth from Wiltshire in 1879 and lived in Cornerswell Road. He was responsible for many of the headstones in St Augustine's churchyard and also for the stone work on many of the town houses.

As the summer of 1916 approached, the people of Britain knew that something big was about to occur in France. The Kitchener Battalions – the renowned New Armies, men who had joined in their thousands in the first months of the war - were about to go into action. And the battle they would fight would give Penarth it's biggest ever loss of life.

Locknagar Crater on the Somme battlefield.

Church life in Penarth was filled with activities and clubs – not least the Boys Brigade.

Chapter Four – The Somme to the Armistice

Well over a thousand men from Penarth enlisted in the army during the Great War, many of them volunteers who joined up during the first two years. In 1916 the "Penarth Parish Magazine" listed 256 men as having joined the colours in that year alone – and that figure included only men in the Anglican Church. It did not even begin to account for men of other denominations.

Despite the fact that 2.5 million men from right across Britain and her colonies had almost immediately volunteered for service in the army, as 1915 progressed the flow of volunteers was reduced to a mere trickle. From the middle of that momentous year it became clear to the War Office that far more than a handful of volunteers would be needed if the war was to be won. Consequently, in January 1916 an Act of Parliament was passed introducing compulsory conscription for all single men over the age of eighteen. In May a further Act legalised the conscription of all married men as well.

By this time there was more than a degree of bitterness and cynicism amongst the veterans of the Western Front. They had fought and bled, seen their comrades killed by German shells, by machine gun fire and by poisonous gas. Yet when they looked at the people back home they saw only well-fed complainers and idlers.

Charles Maunder, from King Street in Penarth, was serving as a private with the 21st Canadian Battalion when he wrote the following poem. It is impossible to read it now without noticing the anger of the foot-slogging soldier, without sensing his bitterness at the conditions he has had to endure while others back home were living a life of ease and comfort:-

Home Thoughts from Abroad

Often in a trench I think
Of the poor chaps at home;
Of the perils that surround them
Wherever they roam.

The train, and train collisions,
The Juggernaut motor cars,
Bacteria in cow's milk
And Zeppelins from afar.

How awful it must be at night
To lie in a feather bed;
To find for breakfast when you rise,
Butter on your bread.

With all these shocking worries
A man's life must be sad;
And to think that I am missing them
Makes me exceeding glad.

Now, out there things are different,
And life here is fancy free;
We have no butter on our bread
Or cow's milk in our tea.

There are no train collisions
Or feather beds at night;
And Zeppelins never trouble us
But keep well out of sight.

And all we have to worry us
Are bullets, bombs and shells;
Bully beef and biscuits
And awful, nasty smells.

So to the chaps in Penarth
I send my sympathy,
And ask them, for their safety,
To come out here with me.

I am only a Penarth boy
But I hope some day to see
Some of the boys from Penarth
In the trenches here with me.

Hardly great poetry but it makes its point! Whether or not it made its point with the people of Penarth is another matter. What is clear is that Maunder and men like him were happy that conscription had now been introduced and that many of the "shirkers" would soon be with them at the front.

Danger was not just the prerogative of men at the front, however, and Penarth Dock saw several deaths during the war years. In January 1916 Norwegian Frank Anderson fell off a ladder that was acting as a gangway onto the SS 'Marina' and smashed his head on the dock wall before dropping into the water. As the Norwegian was reported to be drunk at the time there would undoubtedly have been those who said he got what he deserved. For 16 year old W Morris, a young lad from Windsor Road on his first job with the Penarth Pontoon Company, it was a different matter. He died at the end of February 1916 when a stanchion fell from the ship he was working on and killed him instantly.

Many of the Penarth men who had volunteered in the first two years of the war served with 113 Battery, Royal Garrison Artillery. They had joined the Glamorgan RGA long before the guns of August 1914 jolted the world into harsh reality. To them it meant a little extra money and something to do with their mates on a warm summer's evening. Many Penarth men had connections with the RGA and when 113 Battery was formed at Pembroke Dock on 14th February 1916 dozens of them were transferred to form the nucleus of the new unit – so many, in fact, that it was the closest thing Penarth ever had to a "Pals" Battalion. However, even in the early stages of the war none of them quite realised that their light-hearted quest for a little fun would soon bring them to the brink of death and disaster.

Men of the Royal Garrison Artillery engaged in drill at their Lavernock Camp.

The Battery embarked for France on 12th June 1916 and four days later joined the 31st Heavy Artillery Group, just in time to take part in the bloodbath that became the five month long Battle of the Somme. Gunner Jack Spear had been with 113 Battery since its inception and kept a diary of his movements, whilst in Britain and when abroad. His entries for 12th and 13th June read as follows:-

"12th June
12.30 Arrived Southampton. Guns left Avonmouth same day on board captured German boat, SS 'Hunsgate.'
1.30 Issue of bully beef.
2.30 Embarked on board.
9.40 Left Southampton.
10.00 All had to put lifebelts on.

13th June
1.45 Arrived Rouen
9.00 Arrived in camp."

The RGA pose for a photograph at Lavernock.

Within a few days, however, the unit had moved up to the lines and on Wednesday 20th June Jack Spear was announcing 113 Battery's entry into the war:-

"First shell fired by the 113th Siege Battery at 4.49pm."

A few days later, as the build-up to the battle began in earnest, he reported that:-

"German shrapnel was bursting around us for a quarter of an hour. Shell holes all around. The Battery had gas helmets on – 11.45pm a sudden attack of gas and weeping shells"

The British attack at 7.30 on the morning of 1st July 1916 has gone down in history as the most disastrous episode the British army has ever known. In the first hour of the battle, before most people in Britain had even sat down to breakfast, 16,000 British soldiers died – it was as if the complete population of a town like Penarth, men, women and children alike, had been wiped from the face of the earth. By the end of the day 20,000 had been killed and a further 40,000 had been wounded or posted as missing.

At least 43 Penarth men were killed during the Battle of the Somme which lasted from the beginning of July until the middle of November. Three died on the first day alone, in that suicidal charge across No Man's Land – Frederick Hooper, Charles William Downs and William Tunley. Two Penarth brothers, Leonard and Arthur Tregaskis were killed on the same day, during the assault by the 38th Division, the Welsh Division as it was known, on Mametz Wood between 7th and 12th July. The brothers had left Penarth and emigrated to Canada but on the outbreak of war had returned to their home country to enlist in the Cardiff City Battalion. They now lie buried side by side in the cemetery at Flat Iron Copse, in the menacing shadow of Mametz Wood.

Jack Spear wrote briefly but movingly in his diary about one incident in the Battle of the Somme and it seems to sum up the experiences of many of the 113 boys:-

"We went to man an Observation Post in the close support line, to observe their trenches, and sniper bullets came very near our heads whenever we looked over. All guns were heavily bombarding his trenches all day long for the boys of the Essex Regiment to go over in the evening. At 7.45 pm our guns went all out – it was like Hell let loose as the boys went over. But as soon as our bombardment started Fritz started on our trench with machine guns and 4.2 and 5.9 high explosives, giving us a very hot time, making us run and find a good sap. The strafe lasted about an hour and a half – got back in about 11.00 pm."

One of the many 113 Battery men to die during the Battle of the Somme was Sergeant John Regan who was killed on 31st July. Born on 1st May 1882, by 1916 he was a married man with five children, four boys and a girl. A renowned sportsman, John Regan played for the Penarth Thistle Rugby team and was well known and respected in the Penarth area. Just a week before his death Regan wrote to his wife:-

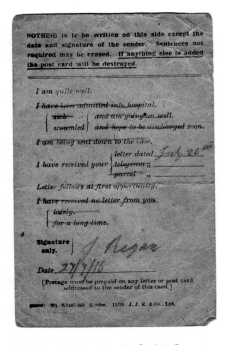

A Field Service Postcard sent by Sgt John Regan to his wife in July 1916.

"I am quite well but sorry I cannot say the same about these, all gone. Sam Thomas of Salop Place got killed yesterday with shrapnel. Lt Whitley, I hear, is killed. Everybody is very sorry for Sam Thomas and Frank Lewis. They were both very nice chaps. I told you in my letter about Frank Lewis. I believe he was gassed and died in no time - - - I have just found the half penny that our little daughter put in the parcel. How thoughtful. I am keeping it for luck."

A few days later he was writing about the battle in which 113 Battery was then involved:-

"The left section advanced our position on the 14th July - - - and picked our position on the right of Montaubon – it proved a very hot position and we vacated it on the 18th after losing Gunner Evans on the 16th and Gunner Francis on the 17th from shell fire. We also lost Gunner F Lewis after an attack of gas on the morning of the 18th. No less than 20 of the section suffered from poison gas."

On the bottom of the letter one of his comrades has written "The writer of this is now dead. Poor chap, Sgt Regan."

John Regan was killed when shrapnel from an exploding shell pierced his chest. He died instantly. In due course, Sergeant Tom Bartlett, another Penarth man, wrote to commiserate with Regan's widow, little knowing that he too would become a casualty that August:-

PENARTH THISTLE RUGBY FOOTBALL CLUB.

Runners up CARDIFF AND DISTRICT LEAGUE. 1903-4. Runners up A. H. WILLIAMS' CUP.

F. SAUNDERS. F. BUTT. W. YOUDE. W. HARTREY. T. TROUGHT (Hon. ?
H. ROWLANDS. A. BRYANT. R. SIMS. J. HOULE. W. DAVIE. T. BLACKMORE.
J. REGAN. F. JAMES. STAN. SMITH (Captain and Secretary). R. GOODMAN. B. LAWDAY.
T. MILES. W. HOOPER.

John Regan, sitting on the left of the second row, is seen here with the other members of the Penarth Thistle Rugby Club, circa 1903-04.

John Regan's original grave in France.

"The war goes on and takes its toll and heavily at times but answering the call of duty our only thought must be for the safety of the loved ones at home - - - Again, our deepest sympathy and with sincere hope that you will be endowed with every power to comfort you in your great loss."

John Regan was buried in Peronne Road Cemetery, a dozen miles to the east of Albert.

"The Penarth Times" for 21st September recorded the death of Tom Bartlett:-

Killed in July 1916, this photograph shows John Regan's modern gravestone.

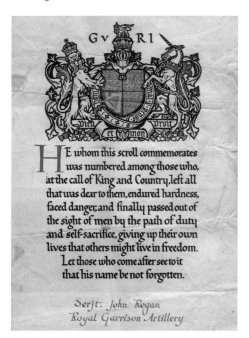

The scroll commemorating John Regan's death – hundreds of similar scrolls were soon to be received by families in Penarth.

"It appears that he, with others, were taking cover in a dugout as the enemy were sending over a few shells, one of which smashed the dugout they were in, killing them all, including Theo Jones of Cogan. Gunner Albert Stamp, Penarth, has written giving particulars of the incident and says 'We buried them next day in the same churchyard as poor John Regan.'"

Bartlett was a well-known bell ringer in the town and on 17th September several scores of Grandsires, Doubles, 720 Bob minors and 240 Kent treble Bob minors were rung at St Augustine's Church, the bells half muffled, in his memory. He was the third Bartlett boy to be killed in the war, his brother Bertie having died in 1914, his younger brother Ernest on 5th May 1916.

That November the Windsor Kinema in Penarth was advertising 'The Battle of the Somme,' the pictorial record of the mighty battle that had been made and distributed with the permission of the British government. A month later, however, the news from the cinema was of a very different kind. "The Penarth Times" for 14th December led with the headline "Who Pinched Charlie?" The article went on:-

"The cut out Charlie Chaplin who has so long stood on guard in the vestibule of the Windsor Kinema was missing from his usual post last week and has not been heard of since. Charlie had been seen outside in the forecourt of the Kinema one night previous to his disappearance and it was suspected then that he had developed wandering habits but it was never thought that he would disappear for good. One report says he was seen skidding along Windsor Road towards the Arcade on one heel but this is unconfirmed."

Penarth merchant seamen continued to be at risk. When the SS 'Borgary' was sunk on Christmas Eve 1916 no fewer than seven of the crew came from the town. Able Seaman William James (King Street) saved the life of Chief Engineer Anderson (Victoria Avenue) as he clung to the side of a swamped lifeboat and the Penarth men spent the next three days adrift before they were picked up by a Norwegian steamer.

Early the following year ship's steward James Matthews was one of only nine survivors when his ship was torpedoed and sunk. Picked up by the U Boat, he was detained on board for a month as the submarine cruised the Western Approaches before returning to her base in Germany. Matthews who came from King Street in the town was then imprisoned for the duration.

The Royal Navy proved to be the undoing of Boy Telegraphist John Morgan Francis when his ship, HMS 'Leforey,' was sunk on patrol off the east coast. He had gone to sea on 8th January 1917 and was killed on 23rd March. He was just 16 years old.

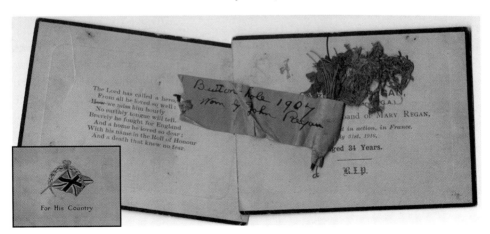

Over 300 Penarth men died in the Great War, a terrible toll when you consider the size of the town.

Another young casualty was Eddy Hookway who had lied about his age and enlisted when he was just 15 years old. Before becoming a soldier Eddy had worked at Glamorganshire Golf Club but within a few months he found himself fighting in the Dardanelles. He had endured two fierce battles before he was seventeen, seeing two comrades shot down on each side of him. Eventually he was invalided home with dysentery and then went to France for 18 months. He was killed before he reached his 19th birthday. His mother was reported as having a dream, seeing him shot, and waking at the exact moment of his death.

For Driver Francis James, however, death was self-inflicted when he shot himself with a comrade's rifle at his billet in Great Yarmouth. His death came as a great shock as he had been at home in Penarth over Christmas and his parents reported him as being in the best of health and spirits. A letter in his pocket was addressed to his mother, stating that he was "broken hearted" and did not know what to do. Unknown to his parents he had recently spent two months in a military hospital due to depression and melancholy. The inquest duly returned a verdict of "Death due to Temporary insanity."

Early in February 1917 an ex soldier was found in a field just outside the town with his throat cut from ear to ear. A blood-stained razor lay at man's side, along with his soldier's discharge book. It transpired that the dead man was Private Arthur Williams from Swansea who had recently been discharged from the Welsh Regiment as being unfit for further duty. Alone, depressed, the man had wandered the roads for several weeks before finally deciding to kill himself.

Two men who were destined not to appear on the town's War Memorial both died at Penarth in 1917. John Benjamin Lye, a ship's steward, came ashore from the SS 'Peerless,' clearly ill but refusing to see a doctor. He had been torpedoed twice, the first time with Germans firing from their U Boat at the survivors as they huddled in the lifeboats. The second time he was adrift for four days. He collapsed on 20th September, a fortnight after coming home, the examining doctor stating that death was caused by heart failure due to the shock of the torpedoing.

Augustin Richard was a French sailor who died on 9th November 1917. His leg became tangled in a coil of rope as his ship, the SS 'St Louis,' was being moved in order to tip coal into Hold Number One. His leg was cut completely off. The crew members quickly found cord and leather and tried to bind it back on but it was hopeless. Richard died from shock and loss of blood before a doctor could be called.

As 1917 wore on food shortages began to make themselves felt in the town. That spring no potatoes could be found, not for love nor money, and grocery shops throughout Penarth were displaying the sign "No Potatoes!" It was a sign of things to come.

The killing fields of the Somme, quiet now but in 1916 and 1917 the graveyard of a nation.

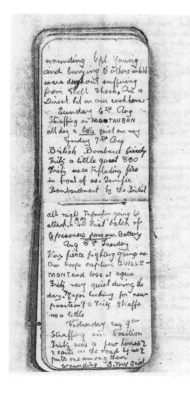

Crime rates continued to rise in the town. At the end of August a Russian merchant ship in the dock was burgled, the thieves managing to escape with a haul of watches, money and other valuables from the crew's quarters. It was a crime the police were unable to solve.

In November the area gained its first Victoria Cross when Captain Richard Wain, from Sully, was posthumously awarded the decoration for his actions while commanding a section of the new-fangled tanks in France. During an assault on the German trenches his tank was disabled by a direct hit and most of the crew killed. Despite being wounded Wain rushed forward with a Lewis machine gun and managed to capture an enemy strong point. He then picked up a rifle and continued to fire at the retreating Germans until he was shot in the head and killed. A member of a well-known Sully family, Wain was commemorated on the family gravestone in Sully Churchyard but not on the Penarth War Memorial.

Jack Spear, the Penarth man who had kept a diary of his activities during the Somme offensive, died on 15th October 1917 during the Third Battle of Ypres – or Passchendale as it is perhaps better known. He had just returned from leave, having spent his time at home in Penarth, and was killed when a British howitzer which was bombarding the enemy trenches blew up. Several men were killed in the explosion, among them Sgt Edward Boyle, also from Penarth. At first Jack Spear was thought only to be injured. He was taken to Base Hospital, however, where he died the following day.

left: Extracts from the diary of Jack Spear.

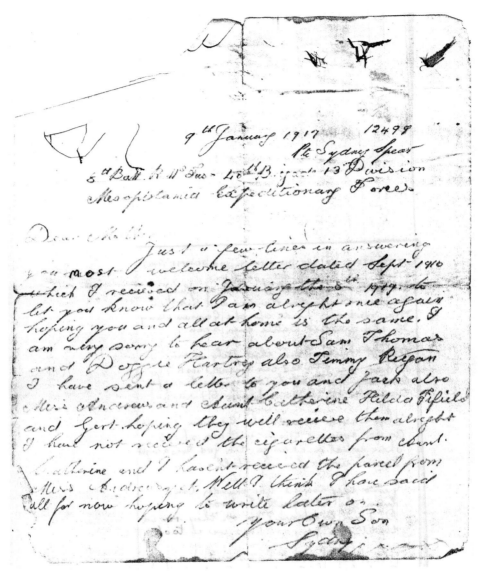

A letter from Jack Spear to his mother, dated 9th January 1917, nine months before he died.

Jack Spear's brother Sydney had been killed the year before, at Gallipoli, in 1916. It is not clear how he died but, in all probability, it was as a result of sniper fire while he was covering the withdrawal of British forces. As if that wasn't enough, the family suffered another loss when their cousin Samuel Spear – also serving in 113 Battery – died on 16th February 1917.

As 1918 dawned there seemed no likelihood of the war ending soon. And the Penarth Food Committee met early in the year in an attempt to formulate a scheme to avoid butter, margarine and meat queues in the town. It was no use. Shortages of food like tea, bacon, butter, jam and meat were soon common and butchers were predicting that it would not be long before the supply was reduced to a quarter a pound of meat per head. It wasn't all bad news, however, and an anonymous writer in "The Penarth Times" was at least able to laugh at the predicament:-

"Oh margarine, oh margarine,
Thy absence causes many a scene.
I stand in queues mid snow and rain
To get some more of Thee again.
Fed up with jam and bloater paste,
Oh Margo come to me in haste!"

WAR LOAN!

THE PENARTH URBAN DISTRICT COUNCIL
desire to strongly urge upon the Inhabitants of the Urban District the great necessity of support-ing the above Loan by every means in their power. It was stated by the Prime Minister recently that the larger the amount subscribed towards the Loan the shorter the War would be. Everybody there-fore should do his or her utmost to bring about this desired end, and thus save the lives of many who are now at the Front.

Applications for Stock to the amount of Five Pounds, or any multiple of Five Pounds, can be made to any Post Office, so that it can be seen that small investors have every opportunity placed before them of assisting in the Loan, and the Council feel that everyone who is in a position to do so, to come forward and help the Country at this period of its need.

As the period for subscribing is short (the last day is on the 16th of February instant) anyone desirous of investing should do so at once.

A. W. MATTHEWS, Chairman of Council.

An advert for War Loans, published in 'The Penarth Times.'

Captain J Watson Black, a Penarth sailor who had been in charge of a large transport during the landings during the Dardanelles campaign, died from typhoid fever on 14th January 1918. He had enjoyed an active war, fighting off a U Boat attack in the Mediterranean, an action for which the Ghurkha officers on board presented him with a jewelled sabre. His ship was later torpedoed at midnight in rough weather and, with great skill, Black successfully managed to get all 600 passengers off the stricken vessel. Latterly he was in charge of hospital ships sailing across the Channel. He was buried in St Augustine's churchyard.

Early in May considerable consternation was caused in the town when call-up notices were sent to several sixteen year old boys. It was an error, however, and the worried youths were quickly told to ignore the summons.

By the late summer of 1918 the Allies were clearly in control of events in France and people's minds were beginning to turn to peace and to ways in which they could commemorate Penarth dead. A Roll of Honour had been kept in St Augustine's Church for several years – the finished memorial, designed by John D Batten, carved in Italian oak, was not finished and dedicated until 1920. In September 1918 a Calvary was erected, as a temporary memorial, at All Saints Church, to the 23 members of the congregation who had fallen in the war.

When peace came to the world on 11th November it was greeted with relief rather than the wild out-pouring of emotion that had greeted the end of the Boer War. Over 300 Penarth men had died in the conflict, a huge proportion of those who had served, considering the size of the town. A committee was promptly appointed by the District Council, their function being to decide on the best way to honour the town's dead.

It was not a task to be taken lightly. Very few streets in Penarth did not have at least one casualty to its name. Some, like Plassey Street, had twenty. Windsor Road had 14, King Street 10. Even small roads like St Augustine's Crescent and Railway Terrace had one while Windsor Arcade in the centre of town had no fewer than three. Twenty two sets of brothers from the town died during the war, four of them being sets of three – the brothers Bartlett, Fitzgerald, Hoult and Northcott. Other sets of brothers such as Oliver and Joseph Hughes fought in the war but, despite being wounded at Mametz Wood, survived the conflict.

Seven Penarth men had died during the first year of war alone while 31 members of the Merchant Navy had perished in the four years of conflict. Six Penarth men died while serving in the Royal Flying Corps, most of them in accidents but some, like Archibald Vincent Shirley, in air combat over Flanders in 1917. The last Penarth casualty was Joseph Kenny of Salop Street who died in hospital at Calais three days after the Armistice was signed.

The war was over at last, the greatest bloodbath the world had ever seen. Now it was time to remember – and time to look to the future.

Penarth Town War Memorial.

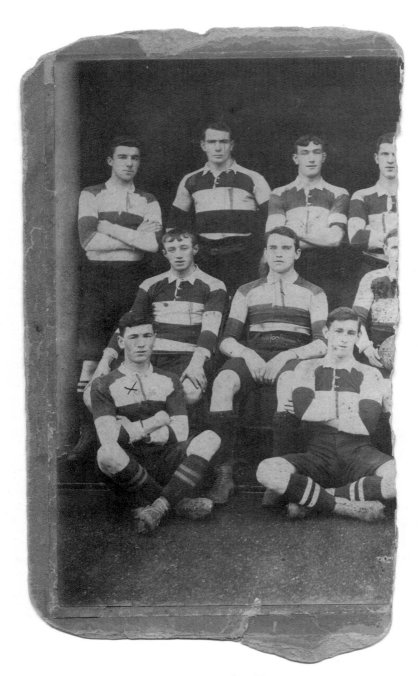

Jack Regan, one of over 300 Penarth men to die in the Great War.

Chapter Five – Between Wars and the Spanish Civil War

Just seven months after the Armistice was signed, in June 1919, the National War Savings Association presented Penarth with a demobilised tank. Crowds lined the streets as the giant metal beast moved slowly up the road from Station Approach towards its final resting place in Alexandra Park. Unfortunately, as it approached Rectory Road the tank came into contact with a lamp post, knocking it down and crushing it – a demonstration, if ever one was needed, of the sheer power and strength of the mighty weapon of war.

Once in position Councillor Sam Thomas, Chairman of the local War Savings Committee, climbed up onto the top of the tank, along with Sir Herbert Corey, MP, and the awesome machine was officially presented to the town as a reminder of the dreadful nature of war. The acceptance and positioning of the tank caused considerable debate in the town, many believing it was too explicit a reminder of the horrors of war but, nevertheless, it stood in Alexandra Park for several years before finally being sold to a firm of scrap merchants for just £45 in May 1937.

The town's War Memorial was formally unveiled on 11th November 1924. Located in Alexandra Park and designed by Sir William Goscombe John, it was made of white granite topped by a bronze winged victory figure standing on a ship's prow and holding a laurel-wreathed sword. On it were listed the names of the Penarth dead and the inscription "These men died for their country. Do ye live for it."

"The Penarth News" of 13th November caught the mood of the moment at the unveiling:-

"In pouring rain, as though the heavens were weeping in memory of the brave men who made the supreme sacrifice, the Penarth War Memorial was unveiled in Alexandra Park on Tuesday by two mothers who had each lost three sons in the war. These were Mrs F Bartlett and Mrs P Fitzgerald."
Mr Hoult, who also lost three sons, had been invited to participate but had declined the offer as he felt it was too painful a reminder of the loss he had suffered. A choir of ex-servicemen sang, lessons were read and a Guard of Honour presented arms to salute the memorial. It was a moving ceremony and many of the crowd, most of whom had lost friends or relatives in the war, were in tears. Immediately the ceremony ended the rain stopped and the sun came out.

Several of the names on the memorial commemorated men and women who had died after the Armistice. Amongst these, the only woman to be listed in the Great War section, was Emily Ada Pickford who was married to one of the owners of "The Penarth Times." A renowned singer and music teacher, she gave over 500 concerts for wounded soldiers during the war years. When the war ended thousands of soldiers were kicking their heels, waiting to be demobilised in France, and Emily was asked if she would become a member of a concert party to help entertain these men. She agreed.

On 7th February 1919 she and her colleagues gave a concert at Guoy in France. Two cars were then provided to transport the party to Abbeville for their next appearance but, unfortunately, their route took them along an icy tow-path at the side of the River Somme. A letter to Emily's family from the famous ventriloquist Tom Burrows, who was in the second car, described what happened:-

"to my horror I saw it (Emily's car) slide over the icy bank into the River Somme. I heard Mr Taylor call 'Help me, I can't swim!' It was very dark and none of the men present seemed to realise at first what had happened. I got nearer to the edge of the water where I saw Miss Nolan, almost exhausted, and I was able to reach out over the river. Fortunately a soldier who had jumped into the water assisted her to the bank. Miss Pickford was never heard nor seen again."

The singer Frederick Taylor also died in the accident. The driver was rescued and later stated that the car had skidded on ice but the Pickford family always believed that he had been drunk and, therefore, a prime cause of the accident.

Lance Corporal George Gallagher of the Inland Water Transport, Royal Engineers, also died in 1919 when he attempted to save the life of a woman he saw fall into the River Seine. He dived in after her but quickly got into difficulties and both he and the woman drowned. Gallagher, who had enlisted in 1915 and served uninjured throughout the war, left a widow and three children back home in Penarth.

Penarth's most famous soldier, and the winner of the town's second Victoria Cross, also died in 1919. This was Samuel George Pearse who had been born in Arcot Street, had lived for many years in Salop Street and had played the French horn in the town's Salvation Army Band. With his parents and brothers, Sam emigrated to Australia in 1911 and in 1915, as soon as he came of age, he enlisted in the Australian Imperial Forces.

The Salvation Army Band, complete with big bass drum, pose happily for the photographer in one of the town's side streets - they certainly couldn't do that today!

Sam Pearse – who was always called George by his wife and mates - saw action in the Dardanelles campaign but by the summer of 1916 he was in France, ready to take part in the Battle of the Somme. He was awarded the Military Medal for his actions during an engagement on the Menin Road and was wounded in the foot at Ville-sur-Ancre in May 1918. He was still on sick-leave when the war ended.

Despite having recently been married, Sam had become used to the military life. So when the opportunity for "a last fling" presented itself he promptly enlisted in the North Russia Expeditionary Force, one of several units fighting on behalf of the White Russians against the Bolsheviks. He was on the troop ship, sailing to Archangel, when he received a letter from his wife Kitty, telling him that she was pregnant. It was enough to convince Sam, who had been thinking about enlisting in a machine gun unit to fight in Mexico, that it was time to settle down. But first there was the Russian campaign to be fought.

They arrived in Archangel on 11th July and marched through dense forests to Emptsa. The Russian Civil War was almost over by now but Sam's unit was ordered to attack a series of blockhouses where the Bolsheviks were waiting. With his platoon pinned down by enemy fire, Sam Pearse cut through the protecting barbed wire, rushed to the side of the building and threw in several Mills bombs. As he moved away an unexpected burst of fire hit him in

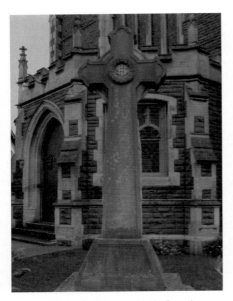

The memorial to the fallen outside the front door of Trinity Church.

the groin. The Bolsheviks had been using Dum-dum bullets and an artery had been severed. As Sam lay on the ground his comrades could do no more than stand and watch as his life blood ebbed away. For his actions that day Sam was awarded the Victoria Cross. His wife Kitty was presented with the medal at a private ceremony in Buckingham Palace in 1920.

One of the town's most unusual war memorials was the J A Gibbs Home in Paget Place. John Angel Gibbs had enlisted as a trooper early in the war. As a member of a prominent ship owning firm there was no obligation for him to join up but he was a man of principle and stated that he would rather die than be thought "a slacker." He was duly commissioned and won the DSO in June 1917. When he was killed on 20th September 1917, leading his Battalion in a charge on the Menin Road, his wife Gladys decided that she would buy the old Taff Vale Railway Hotel and convert it into a home for destitute children as a memorial for her dead husband.

The building was then presented to the National Children's Home and Orphanages, their magazine "Highways and Hedges" for August 1919 declaring that

"The new branch will be used for the education and training of boys for the sea and engineering trades."

The first 27 children took up residence on 24th October 1918. The very first admission was Harold Woodhouse who later went on to a distinguished academic career and was killed

John Angel Gibbs and his wife outside Buckingham Palace on the day he was presented with his DSO.

The Penarth Hotel, purchased by Mrs Gladys Gibbs, presented to NCH and run as a working war memorial, the J A Gibbs Home.

piloting a bomber over Germany during the Second World War. His brother Leslie, the second admission, joined the Royal Navy and achieved the rare distinction of being commissioned from the lower deck. The father of Audrey Batsford, another of the first youngsters to come in, had been killed during the war "by the propeller of a flying machine."

The J A Gibbs Home operated as a nautical training school for many years, one of the country's more useful and realistic war memorials. It changed its name after the Second World War and still runs as Headlands, a school offering care and education for emotionally damaged young people.

With the war against Germany ended, life in Penarth began to return to normal. The pier had taken something of a battering from the soldiers who had requisitioned it for war use – quite apart from anything else, virtually no maintenance had been carried out for several years and the landing stage at the seaward end was in a very poor condition. It meant that the White Funnel paddle steamers were not able to use the pier for several seasons and it was not until April 1926 that the landing stage was open for business once again.

THIS ORGAN WAS ERECTED
TO THE GLORY OF GOD
AND IN MEMORY OF THOSE WHO
FELL IN THE GREAT WAR 1914-1918.

DAVID ABBOTT	ALBERT PAYNE
EDWARD BERESFORD	T. J. POWELL
EDWARD HAYES	WILLIAM RADFORD
CLEMENT HOOPER	PHILEMON RICHARDS
ALFRED HUTCHINS	GEORGE SANDREY
ARTHUR G. MULES	JACK SEARLE
RICHARD PAWLEY	ALBERT SPILLER
W. MELBOURNE LEE	GEORGE STICKLER

The memorial plaque at Albert Road Methodist Church.

In December 1924 the town lost one of its great characters when Police Sergeant William Vaughan was transferred to Treforest. He had been in Penarth for 15 years and during the war had been the Drill Instructor for E Division of the Glamorganshire Police. Vaughan had been in the army before joining the police force and had served with Lord Kitchener in Egypt, and in Crete and China where he was involved in the relief of Peking during the Boxer Rebellion.

In August 1926 the whole town was held riveted for several weeks by "The Penarth Finger Print Case." James Ramsbottom of Cardiff was accused of breaking and entering Cogan Railway Station where he stole seventeen shillings. A piece of broken glass was found to have Ramsbottom's finger prints on it and he was sent to prison for 12 months. The most interesting aspect of the case, however, concerned Ramsbottom's wife who was verbally attacked by the prosecution barrister, demanding to know how many criminal offences she had. She broke down in tears but, despite the issue having no bearing on the case, the barrister was allowed to continue his questioning by the judge.

The Taff Vale Railway Company, previous owners and operators of Penarth Docks, disappeared in the 1922 amalgamation of all the tiny railways that had been operating for years within Britain. Henceforth, the Taff Vale lines would be run by the Great Western Railway – and

The Roll of Honour in St Augustine's Church.

so, too, would its docks. In Wales these included Cardiff and Barry Docks, both of them considerably larger than Penarth. Sooner or later there would have to be a rationalisation and with less and less demand for Welsh coal it was clear that one of the docks would have to close. That was in the future, however, and for the moment Penarth basked in the glow of post-war euphoria.

In 1928 the destroyers 'Velox' and 'Walker' paid a courtesy visit to the town. A civic reception was held for the officers and the two crews were given free entry to the pier and the Windsor Kinema. The two ships were opened to the public and thousands flocked on board to squeeze down companionways and ladders and generally enjoy the experience of being on board these wonderful new ships.

On 14th June 1928 an estimated crowd of 50,000 people thronged the sea front to watch Sir Alan Cobham try to land his flying boat on the Bristol Channel. The sea was too rough, however, and he was forced to touch down instead on Cardiff Bay. When the news of Cobham's new destination was given, thousands rushed up the hill and through the Kymin to watch the landing. At 3.00 pm Cobham took off again and flew low over the Esplanade before heading off to Southampton.

By the end of 1928, out of a total population of about 19,000, there were over 1000 unemployed men in Penarth. When, in April of the following year, the Great Western Railway closed its locomotive shed at Penarth Docks another 150 men were thrown out of work. It did not bode well for the future.

There was some light relief in the town, however. In the summer of 1928 mixed bathing was at last allowed in the town baths and dozens of young people poured into the pool to enjoy the unusual experience.

In October Mrs Esther Harris donated a double-fronted clock for the new pavilion that had been built on the landward end of the pier. The clock was to commemorate her son Stewart (Solly) who had been killed on 26th August 1915 during the Great War. Despite being previously wounded, Solly had returned to the trenches and subsequently died in close quarter fighting. His funeral was conducted by a Jewish officer, the exact spot of the grave marked so that a Jewish memorial could later be erected at the place.

By the summer of 1936 war clouds were beginning to loom once more and an open air meeting of the local Fabian Society near Bridgeman Road was attended by over 100 interested people. The speakers deplored the breaking down of the League of Nations and urged the following of collective security.

At the end of July 1936 a party of Hitler Youth boys came to the town, on a cycling tour through Britain. The group was apparently given a "hearty welcome" and stayed in the area for two days. In hindsight it is, perhaps, a little too easy to imagine ulterior motives behind the visit. Suffice to say that the German Consul joined the young people as they sat around a bonfire and entertained people with English and German folk songs.

There were more pressing concerns for the people of Penarth, however, as the GWR was soon announcing what everyone in the town had feared and half expected for years - the closure of Penarth Dock:-

"Notice is hereby given that on Monday 6th June 1936, and until further notice, vessels will not be admitted into Penarth Dock for the purpose of loading or discharging, nor will any traffic be dealt with at that dock."

It was a simple, blunt message, one that brooked no argument. On 4th July the last ship, the 'Amiens,' left the docks. "The Penarth Times" watched her go:-

When Penarth Docks closed in 1936 it spelt economic disaster for the town.

"True to their traditions, the dockers loaded 2249 tons of coal in fourteen and a half hours of actual loading and at 12.25 am on Saturday, like a ghost ship slipping her moorings, the 'Amiens' silently passed through the gates for the open sea, while the chill stillness of the dreary grey morning was broken only by the raucous cry of the gulls and the heavy sighs of those who had loaded probably their last vessel."

Only the drab grey outline of the Greek steamer 'Antonios' remained. She had been abandoned beneath a coal tip and was likely to remain there for some time to come. The men who for years had worked on the dock packed up their tools and possessions and headed home for the last time. The docks had closed and there was very little prospect of them opening again.

Soon, however, the battered 'Antonios' was joined in the empty dock by another vessel. This was the Spanish ship 'Duero' which was at Cardiff when General Franco and his Fascists rose in revolt against Spain's Republican Government. The ship's owners refused to accede to the government's request to increase the wages of the crew and so she was stuck in Wales. To keep her in Cardiff, however, was expensive and so the 'Duero' was moved to Penarth where she was berthed alongside a jetty. Her full crew was on board but as they were being paid no wages they had little chance to enjoy the delights of the seaside town.

It was not long before another Spanish ship, the 'Arinda-Mendi,' was brought to Penarth Dock and London newspapers quickly picked up on a rumour that the two ships had been commandeered by the "Spanish Left." Soon, went the rumour, they would be sailing for Spain, their holds full of machine guns and aeroplane parts for the forces of the "Left" in its fight against Franco. It was a rumour without any substance.

The tourist trade provided some measure of comfort for the people of Penarth once the docks closed.

The Spanish Civil War had broken out in July 1936 and did not end until January 1939. Nearly a million people were killed in the war and both sides committed hideous atrocities. Germany and Italy immediately gave support to Franco's Fascists, using the war as a dress rehearsal for the bigger, wider war they were planning. Soviet Russia offered help to the Republicans and 40,000 volunteers from many different countries formed themselves into an International Brigade to fight on the Republican side. Amongst them were several Penarth men.

On 25th February 1937, "The Penarth Times" ran an article under the headline 'Penarth Man Fighting for Spain':-

"Harold Paterson, a 29 year old Penarth welder, of 26 Maughan Street, who left home just after Christmas in the SS 'Stanhope,' bound for Barcelona, has written home to his parents informing them that he has joined the British section of the Loyalist Army in Spain."
Paterson was something of a wanderer, having worked all over the world in a whole variety of different jobs. Before leaving for Spain he had joked with his father, telling him not to be surprised if he decided to "join up" while out there. The next thing his family knew a letter arrived, telling them that he had joined the International Brigade.

A few weeks later Lester Evans from Arcot Street received a letter from Paterson, stating that he had been wounded in action. The wound, however, was not serious:-

"Have dodged the bullet and will soon be back again killing Fascists."

Just a month later thirteen year old schoolboy David Deere went missing from his Penarth home. His mother was convinced that the boy had been lured to Spain by the "recruitment organisation for the Red Army." The boy had been last heard of on a cycling holiday but when his two friends returned to the town David was not with them. In the end David Deere was traced to Devon where, fascinated by the military, he had enlisted in the Suffolk Regiment. He was duly sent back home.

In May 1937 a Penarth man, Able Seaman Tom Eley, was a member of the crew of HMS 'Hunter' when she was mined off the coast of Spain. The destroyer had been involved in convoying Spanish refugees to Gibraltar when she struck the mine. Four crewmen were lost but Tom Eley was amongst those saved. His telegram home to Penarth was brief but pertinent – "All safe. Tom." A letter he sent to his parents after he reached Gibraltar was a little more explicit:-

HMS 'Hunter,' decks awash after she struck a mine during the Spanish Civil War.

The remains of the galley on board HMS 'Hunter.' Penarth sailor Tom Eley was lucky to survive the explosion.

"I don't know how to tell you what really happened, I don't want to be in anything like it again. I was down below, asleep, when whatever hit us exploded and that was followed by the boiler blowing up - - - What made things worse was that the entrance onto the Mess Deck was blown up and on fire so we had to get on deck, one at a time, through the ammunition hoist. - - - The ship was going over onto her side all the time so after the injured were got into the boats we were ordered to Abandon Ship. I was picked up by a Spanish destroyer with about twenty others."

That was not the end of Tom Eley's adventures. He was one of a dozen seamen who volunteered to return to the stricken destroyer and crew her as she was towed, stern first, to port. Despite being only 150 miles distant it still took 24 hours to reach Gibraltar, working the pumps all the way. With half her bottom blown out it is a wonder any of them made it. Four years later Tom was not so fortunate, being one of Penarth's first casualties during the Second World War.

There were several significant issues for the town in 1937. Firstly, there was the Coronation of the new king, George V1. Penarth had always had a soft spot for the new monarch, ever since he had visited the town, when he was the Duke of York, in 1921. On 27th July he had officially opened the J A Gibbs Home before visiting the Seaman's Mission in the docks and the town's Ex-Service Men's Club. On the occasion of his Coronation the town was decked with bunting and there were several street parties. For some reason, however, there seemed to be no bonfires – always a tradition in the town – for these celebrations.

One of the old cannons that stood in Penarth for many years.

The other momentous event that year was the removal of the old tank that had stood for nearly two decades in Alexandra Park. The Editor of "The Penarth Times," in his "Silurian – Topical Talks" column, deplored the removal of the tank and the old Crimean War vintage cannons that had also graced town parks:-

"There are quite a number of Penarth residents who will be sorry to see the tank and guns leave Alexandra Park and Windsor Gardens. Grim as they may be as deadly instruments of war, they have occupied honoured positions amid the flowers and shrubbery for so many years that Penarth folk have come to regard them with no little measure of sentiment."

Many Penarth merchant seamen were involved in the Spanish Civil War, dozens of them regularly making the run from South Wales to ports like Barcelona. In June 1937 Messrs G H Hazard and M F Bellamore were members of the crew of the SS 'Jeanne M' when she was shelled, from a direction they least expected it:-

"We were awakened by the bursting of heavy shells close to the steamer. Everyone was looking for planes but we soon found that the shells were coming from seaward."

Unwittingly, they had blundered into the path of a German naval force that was bombarding the town of Almeria. Over 200 shells were fired and soon the town was blazing. The Penarth sailors, however, managed to escape.

Others were not so lucky. In August 1937 Captain W G Bullock, of Stanwell Road, and his ship, the SS 'African Trader,' were bombed by Spanish Nationalist aircraft while lying in Gijon Harbour. While there no casualties, the ship was holed and had to be beached for repairs. A year later Bullock was again attacked. By now he was skipper of the 'Brisbane' and this time he and six of his crew were killed when Nationalist aircraft bombed and machine gunned the merchant ship. Bullock's body was never recovered from the blazing wreck and the survivors were machine-gunned as they were making for the shore in their lifeboats.

At this stage of the war Penarth men were already returning from Spain, telling tales about the incredible barbarity of the conflict. William Pemberton, chief engineer of the 'Essex Lance,' had been forced to spend a month ashore in Barcelona and had been sickened by the dead bodies he had seen strewn across the roads after air raids.

Fred Croll, of Windsor Road, was clear – he would not be returning to Spain, not for double the wages! His ship, the Royal Mail steamer 'Nela,' had been on charter to the Spanish Government, carrying meat from Argentina to Barcelona. Most of that meat was promptly sent to the front, he said, very little of it finding its way to the starving women and children of the country. In a 32 hour period in the city, Croll witnessed no fewer than 16 air raids. Most of these were directed against the residential areas, the Nationalists taking care not to damage the valuable docks. While in Barcelona Fred Croll had also met and spoken with another Penarth man, Ronald Peters of Archer Terrace, who was then fighting with the International Brigade.

When the SS 'African Mariner' – sister ship to the ill-fated 'African Trader' – was bombed in October 1938, the Penarth skipper, P H Manley, found himself arrested on a charge of smuggling Spaniards out of the war zone and taking them to France. After a week or so in jail Manley was released and returned to Penarth, much to the relief of his wife and daughter who had spent the time worrying and wondering if they would ever see him again.

Meanwhile, back in the town, the stories of air raids and the destruction caused to Spanish cities were making the people of Penarth think about their own safety should war come once more to Britain. Thanks to the rapid development of bomber aircraft, this time everybody would be in the front line. Although the docks had been closed in 1936, should war be declared they would probably have to be opened again and that meant the town would become an immediate target for enemy bombers.

It was estimated that Penarth would require at least 200 Air Raid Precaution Wardens and volunteers were needed from the men and women of the community. An appeal by the District Council saw dozens of applications come flooding in. Such volunteers, for posts like Special Constables, ARP Wardens and Auxiliary Fire Fighters, were enrolled and put through basic and rudimentary training. On one occasion the police Specials were run through a makeshift gas chamber, albeit wearing respirators, housed in a van at the back of the police station – they would undoubtedly have been unaware of the poignant irony in the fact that gas vans like this were how Hitler's murder chambers first began. The threat of gas attack was a major pre-occupation at that time, a poem in "The Penarth Times" soon warning:-

Cadets from the Gibbs Home prepare for a fancy dress parade.

"If you get a choking feeling and a smell of musty hay
You can bet your bottom dollar that there's phosgene on the way.
But the smell of bleaching powder will inevitably mean
That the enemy you're meeting is the gas we call chlorine."

It was a ghoulish pre-occupation but a real one nonetheless. ARP trenches were also dug on places like Cogan fields but due to the nature of the soil - always liable to flooding in wet weather - they were never really successful.

Basque refugee children visited the town in January 1939 but because of wet weather and a water-logged playing field they were unable to enjoy the football and outdoor games they had been promised. Instead they were restricted to playing indoor games in Stanwell Road Baptist Schoolroom where, in the evening, they later gave a concert of singing and Spanish dancing.

Anti-Semitism reared its ugly head in the town early in the year when a Jewish businessman, Mr Benjamin Robinson, arrived on board his motor launch moored in Penarth Dock only to find a swastika flag and a message nailed to the deck – "Your tribe is a big enough nuisance on land. Be warned and keep off the sea." It seems to have been an isolated incident, however, and there was no repetition.

By the beginning of 1939 International Brigade forces had been withdrawn from the war zones of Spain and, on 15th February, Bob Peters who lived in Archer Terrace and had just returned from a year-long stint as despatch rider with the force, gave a talk at the Public Lecture Room of the town library. He spoke movingly about the suffering of the women and children caught in the conflict – it was estimated that 300,000 Spanish children would be starving by the end of the year.

Bob Peters had been born in Penarth in November 1914, one of nine children who were raised by their mother. His father had disappeared, presumed killed, during the Great War. After leaving Albert Road Boys School, Bob worked for a time as a shop assistant and then milkman in the town before emigrating to Canada in 1931. When the Spanish Civil War broke out he travelled 4500 miles to fight with the International Brigade. He officially became a "brigader" when he was issued with his pay-book in the bullring at Albacete.

Acting as a runner for Brigade HQ, Bob was shot and wounded when his unit was pinned down in a dry river bed during the Battle of Brunete in July 1937. The ambulance that took him to hospital had no spare bunks and he had to stand all the way, in agony the whole time. When he arrived at hospital they found that the bullet was lodged against his spine and was in too dangerous a position to operate. So they simply left it where it was!

While recuperating Bob Peters heard that drivers of all types were needed and as he owned and drove a motorcycle back home in Canada he decided to volunteer as a despatch rider. He spent the rest of the war careering around Spain on battered Gilera and Motobocane bikes. He was repatriated in 1938 and came back to Penarth to see his family.

More immediate events were beginning to impinge upon the town, however. Hitler had been appeased for far too long and, slowly but inevitably, the world was being drawn into war once more. As with the Great War, twenty five years earlier, the people of Penarth were prepared to play their part.

Sketches
of Tommy's life
Up the line — N° 8   Waiting for the barrage to lift. It makes you feel small and sort of lost !

A humorous look at the war.

VIEW IN ALEXANDRA PARK, PENARTH, SHOWING GUNS. No.1076.

Crimean War Cannon in Alexandra Park.

WINDSOR GARDENS. PENARTH.

Elegant Penarth.

Flight Sergeant Arthur James, with his squadron, sitting second from the right in the front row.

sunset and one hour after sunrise – the Magistrate warned them that any repetition of such behaviour would see them both being sent to prison. The pair claimed to have been fishing but the arresting officer stated that he had clearly smelled alcohol on their breath.

In April 1941 Donald Leslie Hooper, a member of the RAF, was sent for trial at the next Quarter Sessions, charged with breaking and entering a number of houses in Penarth while in September four Scottish soldiers posted to the town robbed Airman John Llewellyn of his watch, cigarettes, lighter, railway ticket and £9 in money. When appearing before the bench their only defence was that the airman had jostled them, dropped his watch and then ran away! In January 1942 Idwal Davies was fined £5 for speeding through Penarth and Dinas Powis during the black out. Police evidence said that he had reached speeds of between 24 and 44 mph!

Penarth sailors in the Merchant Navy continued to court danger. Their war was an un-heroic one but its successful conclusion was essential if Britain was to survive the immediate threat and make it through the conflict. And the list of MN ships sunk and sailors killed continued to grow throughout the war. Harold Toye of Windsor Road was one of 20 survivors when his ship was torpedoed in April 1941. Married only a few months before, Toye was afloat in an open boat for four days before being picked up by a Dutch merchantman. Toye had been lucky. In just one issue of the paper, "The Penarth Times" for 26th June 1941 listed three Penarth men who had died at sea – Bert Tongs and Ronald Wilson, who had gone down on the same ship, and Ernest John McIver.

By January 1942 the Council was debating the state of bomb damage in the town. The Town Surveyor was quite clear on the matter. The Ministry of Home Security had already issued a statement - bomb sites could only be cleared if they were a danger to public health. Fulminate as they might, the Council could do nothing.

The Penarth Home Guard suffered a fatality early in January when Frank Francis of Church Place South collapsed in the lane at the rear of his house in the early hours of the morning. "The Penarth Times" commented:-

"It appears that Mr Francis left the house at about 5.30 am to go on Home Guard duty, which was to bring in men from their outposts. He was in company with another Home Guard, Mr S Rosser, whom he left at about 7 o'clock and was returning home and had reached the lane at the rear where he apparently collapsed."

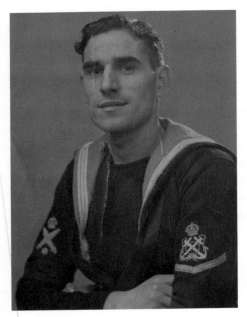

Petty Officer Harry Bowden, drowned when his submarine was rammed and sunk by a Canadian escort vessel in 1942.

Francis had been found and carried into his house by two policemen but died soon afterwards.

More Penarth casualties were to come. On Sunday 21st June 1942 submarine P514 was run down and sunk with all hands off the coast of Newfoundland. On board was Penarth man Harry Bowden. The P514 had left the American Naval Base at Argentina for St John's on the afternoon of 20th June, escorted by the corvette 'Primrose.' Visibility was poor and the following day the submarine found herself in the path of a small convoy escorted by the Canadian minesweeper 'Georgian.' The minesweeper sighted the low, sleek shape of P514 and, putting her engines to full ahead, immediately rammed her amidships on the port side. The submarine healed over, her navigation lights flickered on and then she sank from view.

There was no time to shut watertight doors so the question of using escape devices was immaterial. Within moments everyone on board was dead. The search for survivors went on for three days but it was no use. The P514 had gone down with all hands.

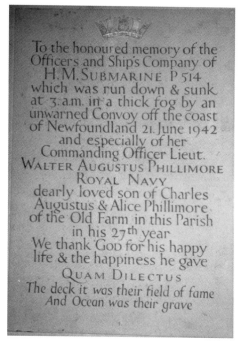

To the honoured memory of the
Officers and Ship's Company of
H.M. SUBMARINE P 514
which was run down & sunk
at 3 a.m. in a thick fog by an
unwarned Convoy off the coast
of Newfoundland 21. June 1942
and especially of her
Commanding Officer Lieut.
WALTER AUGUSTUS PHILLIMORE
ROYAL NAVY
dearly loved son of Charles
Augustus & Alice Phillimore
of the Old Farm in this Parish
in his 27th year
We thank GOD for his happy
life & the happiness he gave
QUAM DILECTUS
The deck it was their field of fame
And Ocean was their grave

A memorial to the men of submarine P514 and her commanding officer, Lt Phillimore, in Swinbrook Church, Oxfordshire.

Harry Bowden was a Petty Officer Torpedo Gunners Mate who had joined the navy in 1936 and later volunteered for service in submarines. He had travelled to Canada by passenger ship in order to join his boat, as submarines are always called. Quite possibly he had a "pier head jump," sailor's language for going to a submarine at the last moment to replace someone who had gone sick or left the boat in a hurry. If that was the case he was decidedly unlucky in his posting.

Harry came from a well-known Penarth family. They were originally from the Grangetown area of Cardiff and moved to Penarth to open a bakers shop in the 1920s. In all there were eleven brothers and sisters living in the Penarth area, Harry's elder brother, Herbert, going on to become a Privy Councillor, Lord President of the Council and Secretary of State for Commonwealth Affairs.

Harry's daughter, Janet West, was just three years old when her father died:-

"I don't remember an awful lot about him. I just remember that he was a sailor who was going to come home and see me. When he died they tried to tell me he wouldn't be coming back. They had a Hell of a job, trying to convince me, because he had said he was coming back and that's what I believed."

Harry Bowden with his wife and daughter, at home in Penarth.

The loss of submarine P514 was a tragic accident. Apart from the escorting 'Primrose' no-one knew she was at sea and when the 'Georgian' sighted a submarine in the water ahead of her it was naturally assumed that it was a U Boat. Harry Bowden, like the rest of the crew of P514, has no known grave but he is remembered on the Penarth War Memorial and on the naval memorial at Plymouth.

Military honours came to Penarth when Squadron Leader Thomas Frederick Dalton, son of Mr T R Morgan of Plymouth Road, was awarded a DFC and Bar. A renowned night fighter ace, Dalton's citation read:-

"He has displayed exceptional skill, both as a squadron commander and an individual fighter during two consecutive nights - - - when he destroyed three enemy aircraft, bringing his total victories to thirteen."

On a more mundane but equally practical note, "The Penarth Times" for 10th July 1942 was reporting about the opening of a new British Restaurant in Windsor Arcade. With Lord Woolton estimating that 94 million meals were eaten away from home each year, like all British Restaurants the aim of the establishment was to offer cheap but good quality food and save on the cost of gas and electricity in the home:-

"The restaurant is over the old Cash and Carry Kitchen and is attractively furnished with tables for four and comfortable folding chairs."

By December 1942 the restaurant was proving to be one of the most popular eating places in town. In November alone 5119 meals had been served and the figure, it was estimated, was rising steadily.

America had entered the war in December 1941 and with American troops now arriving in Britain in huge numbers, Thanksgiving Day of 1942 was celebrated in style in Penarth. There is no doubt that Penarth and Cardiff saw their fair share of "Yankee" visitors and, with most of them being unable to spend the day as a holiday, a dance was arranged in the Marina Ballroom at the end of Penarth Pier. The event was judged to be a great success and as the year came to a close it really did seem as if events were, to quote Prime Minister Winston Churchill, reaching "the end of the beginning."

Soldiers off to war - a scene repeated throughout Britain.

VE day brought celebrations to the town.

Chapter Seven – The Beginning of the End

The year 1943 did not start too propitiously for Penarth. One early morning in January a rowing boat capsized in the dock and eight men were thrown into the water. Six of them managed to swim to safety but Captain Graves and his son Frank were seen to be in difficulties. Arthur Curtin was working on the dockside, saw what was happening and plunged into the water. He managed to locate both men and, for a while, keep them afloat. As he grew weaker, however, he was forced to let go of the older man and Captain Graves sank from sight. Curtin managed to pull Frank back to shore and was duly awarded the parchment testimonial of the Royal Humane Society for his bravery.

"The Penarth Times" for 11th March gave notice of a rare sighting in the town – a banana:-

"Many Penarth people must have seen a real banana for the first time for some years. In the window of Messrs Jessies in Windsor Road, there is the prized fruit, bringing back to the large number of people who have gazed at it reminiscences of pre-war days when bunches of those ripe, yellow bananas hung in all the greengrocers shops."

This was a "patriotic" banana, however, as it was helping with the war effort. Collected on one of his trips abroad - and then jealously guarded all the way home - by Mr Toms, a merchant seaman from the town, the banana, along with two lemons and three oranges, was to be raffled, the proceeds being donated to the Wings for Victory Campaign.

April 1943 saw an inquest, at Penarth Police Station, into the death of Robert Snowden, an RAF Warrant Officer who had committed suicide. On 8th April Snowden attended a dance at the town's Masonic Hall and then, just after midnight, returned to his room in the Sergeants Mess in Rectory Road. There he shot and killed himself. His wife gave evidence at the inquest, saying that although they had been married for eight years he had recently sent her a letter saying that he was depressed and in love with another woman. This woman came from London and, it was claimed, was pregnant. Snowden, in his own way, was another of the many casualties of war.

The Gibbs Home lost fifteen of its old pupils during the conflict – their names are commemorated on a brass plaque set on a lectern that was, for many years, held in the school chapel. Amongst the dead were youngsters like Ronald Gunter, a galley boy on the SS 'Daydawn,' and Albert Andrews, a Mess Room Boy on the MV 'Glenmoor.' The two boys were 15 and 16 years old respectively. Charles Leeds was the Chief Officer of the SS 'Menin

Trinity Church, well used by servicemen during the war.

Ridge.' He died early in the war, on 24th October 1939, when his ship was torpedoed. There were only five survivors.

Also included on the Gibbs Home Memorial was Flying Officer Harold Woodhouse who had gone on from the Home to a brilliant academic career at Cardiff and Cambridge Universities. Having joined the RAF at the start of the war Harold Woodhouse was killed when the Lancaster bomber he was piloting was shot down over Germany on the night of 25th/26th May 1943.

Although most of the Gibbs Home boys were not Penarth residents by birth, they had all spent a considerable period of their lives in the town. The Home – and its young residents – had been accepted as an important part of the community and their deaths were mourned throughout the town.

By 1942 Penarth Docks was playing a vital role in the war effort. Most of the exports from the docks that year were destined for the North African campaign but also in 1942 the Royal Engineers set up a training base at Penarth for their Dock Operations Units. With a view to helping docks and ports continue working after enemy bombing raids but also with half an eye to the future, when Allied forces might land once more in Europe, men were trained to operate damaged dock instillations. The key was learning how to improvise and operate quickly, under very difficult conditions.

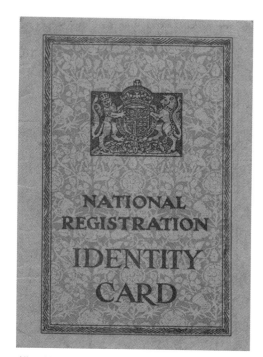

All residents of Penarth had to hold Identity Cards like this one during the war years.

The plaque commemorating the fact that Guy Gibson once stayed at No 2 Archer Road, Penarth.

A training unit was established on the South Quay, complete with derricks and winches and even an old cargo vessel to practise on. Four lighters were provided and over 5000 men passed through the course which included things like learning how to load and unload lighters and how to transfer materials between lighters and larger merchant ships.

The famous Guy Gibson, leader of the Dam Buster raids, became a public personality in May 1943. With the success of the daring, low level raids on the Ruhr dams Gibson's face was quickly plastered across the national newspapers, all of them desperate for a hero to acclaim. As Paul Brickhill has said

"Gibson looked the part; Gibson and glamour were indivisible."

His Penarth connection came in the shape of his wife, the actress Eve Moore, who lived with her parents in Archer Road. Gibson was a regular visitor to the town and the day that the news of the raids broke Eve had the shock of her life, opening the papers and finding her husband's photograph splashed across the pages. The missions had been top secret and throughout all the long months of training and planning Gibson had simply told her that he had been "resting" at a flying school.

There was a memorable celebration in the clubhouse of the Glamorganshire Golf Club – where Eve's father was a member – when

Guy Gibson was duly awarded the Victoria Cross for his courageous leadership of 617 Squadron and his actions during the Dam Buster raids. And a few months later both Guy and Eve were elected life members of the club as a mark of appreciation for services to his country.

Sadly, it was a privilege the flyer was never to enjoy. In an effort to stop the glamorous hero flying any more dangerous missions Winston Churchill took him to America on a "show the flag" tour and, on his return, made sure he was given a desk job. Gibson was not happy and managed to persuade his senior officers to allow him a few last missions. On 19th September 1944 he took off in a Mosquito fighter-bomber to lead a raid on a factory at Rheydt on the Ruhr. His guided in the bombers and his last radio message was "OK chaps, that's fine. Now beat it for home."

Gibson never returned, crashing into a low hill in Holland. The cause of his death is unknown but he was probably brought down by anti-aircraft fire.

Another town hero who died that year was Hugh Jones who was a Sapper on bomb disposal duties with the Royal Engineers. He came from a renowned Penarth family, his mother being the daughter of Penarth's old fire brigade captain Richard Meazey. Sapper Jones had been involved in the Dunkirk evacuation when the ship on which he was being transported was hit by a German bomb. He survived and on his return to Britain volunteered for bomb disposal work but was killed on 30th September 1943 when the bomb he was disarming exploded.

Penarth was not always full of heroes, however, and on 27th May 1943 Arthur Prince of Salop Street was sent to prison for 14 days for failing to attend any Home Guard parades for the previous two years. Apparently the young man had lost his job and spent most of his time loafing on the Billybanks, excusing himself from parades because of "a pain in his side."

A US Navy Base was established in the docks on 26th October 1943 and formally commissioned on 13th January the following year. Under the command of Amphibious Bases, UK, the 11th Amphibious Force took over a large part of the dock as a servicing and repair base for amphibious craft. The Americans quickly built workshops for fitting out and repair of landing craft but also recreation rooms and kitchens in order to supply their troops. An Officers Club was established in Beach Road and junior officers were quartered at 9 Clive Crescent.

In an attempt to shorten the route between Northcliff House and their base in the docks, the Americans built a massive wooden stairway from the top of the cliff down to the side of the old Custom House, a hundred feet below. Known as Jacob's Ladder, the stairway survived the American occupation of the docks but was demolished when the war ended in 1945.

Penarth in the war years, the photograph being taken by John Randall while he was home on leave.

Nearly 150 landing craft, including 70 huge Landing Craft (Tanks), were serviced in Penarth Dock and after the Salerno landings many damaged vessels were brought to the base for repair. Roy Thorne has said:-

"On one occasion 56 amphibious craft were lying in the dock with their numbers on their bows covered by blue plywood to hide their identity."

These craft were ready and prepared, waiting for the D Day landings which finally took place on 6th June 1944. Over twenty small coasters were also harboured in the dock at that time, loaded with ammunition for the invasion and from then on a continual stream of merchant ships sailed from Penarth, supplying the armies in Europe.

The US Penarth base was closed in July 1944, transferring its operations to the Mediterranean as part of General Patton's landings in the south of France. The US Navy clearly regretted the move, Roy Thorne quoting from "The History of the US Navy Bases in the UK":-

"As this was not only one of the best repair establishments but also one of the very few places in the entire command where LSTs could be taken alongside for repair, its loss was seriously felt and soon apparent."

The Americans had certainly made their presence felt in the town, being regularly seen in the streets where they quickly made friends with the local children – "Got any gum, chum" was a phrase often heard – and with the unattached girls. A real taste of the USA was brought to the County School playing field at the end of July 1943 when American troops played a game of baseball before a bemused crowd of some 400 Penarth residents. For two hours the locals were kept enthralled and entertained but many of them went away at the end of the game knowing little more about the sport than they had done at the beginning of the day.

American troops were again bemusing the locals that September. "The Penarth Times" for 16th of the month commented that:-

"People on the beach on Thursday witnessed a very interesting incident. At about 2-o-clock a motor boat was seen speeding along the Channel and in it were what seemed to be four soldiers. Onlookers were watching the manoeuvres of the craft when it suddenly headed straight for the shore and in a few seconds was hauling itself onto dry land."

What people were watching was one of the new DUCKW's, multi-purpose amphibious craft that had been used in the recent invasion of Sicily and in the Pacific. As watchers gazed in amazement the machine drove up the beach, along the Esplanade and disappeared up Cliff Hill.

Several Penarth women had enlisted or been called up for service during the war and on 23rd October 1943 Louisa Jane Kulke, a Lance Corporal in the ATS, died in an accident while on a gas course at Salisbury. A well-known figure in the Penarth area, Louisa had been cashier at the Washington Theatre for two years and was the first Penarth woman to be killed on active service.

Another Penarth woman, Dorothy Pauline Guy who had gone to work in London as a masseuse, was killed on 18th June 1944. One of Hitler's new wonder weapons, a V1 flying bomb, hit the Guards Chapel at Wellington Barracks where she happened to be at the time and killed her outright. Another Penarth woman, the writer Elizabeth Sheppard-Jones, was seriously injured and disabled in the incident.

In December 1943 Major S T Evans, the man who had formed the Penarth Home Guard, retired due to ill-health. He was succeeded by Captain Stanley but the days of the Home Guard were numbered and with the threat of invasion well and truly laid to rest they were "stood down" a year later on 3rd December 1944.

"COR! PARATROOPS!!"

The Home Guard was originally intended to defend the country against paratroops. Formed in 1940, these part-time soldiers served faithfully until all Home Guard units were stood down in December 1944.

Another Evans, this time Sub Lt David Evans, son of Lt Colonel S T Evans of Victoria Square, was in the news at the end of March 1944 when he spoke on German radio. His voice was heard to say "Hello all at home. I hope you are all as well as I am." When asked by the German announcer how he was getting along he replied that he had no complaints. It might not have been Lord Haw-Haw but there is no doubt the Nazi party gained some degree of publicity from the brief appearance of Sub Lt Evans.

A new craze hit Penarth in May 1944 – the theft of American jeeps. Noel Price, a Cardiff boy, came across one of the vehicles in the town and leapt in. Challenged by a sentry he refused to stop and six revolver shots were fired at the jeep, shattering the windscreen. The boy then tried to run police off the road before being forced to a halt. Amazingly, he was fined only £5 for the offence. There was another jeep theft the following week and this time, fearing an epidemic was about to break out, the Magistrates sent the offender to an Approved School.

News of the D Day landings brought a great stir to the town. Everyone had been expecting it but the waiting, particularly for those who had sons involved in the affair, had been almost unbearable. When the news broke several of the town's churches opened their doors and hundreds poured inside to prey. One of the Penarth men taking part in the invasion was Lt David Knapp who went ashore in one of the mine destroying tanks – the "funnies" as they were called – in the first wave. He was wounded during the landing but recovered after a brief period in hospital. On 10th August came the news that Lance Corporal Donald Boulton of Andrew Road had been awarded the Military Medal for his bravery during the landings, the first Penarth man to be awarded a decoration for operations in France after D Day.

In August 1944 the town took in 129 evacuees, mainly children from London fleeing the new flying bomb threat. After arriving in Penarth they were given a meal at the British Restaurant and then billeted amongst the people of the town.

The wedding of one of the town's greatest heroes, Flight Lieutenant Nigel Lidgett Gibbs DFM, took place on 25th August. He had won his DFM flying as an observer in the North African campaign when he and his pilot, Fl Lt Etherton, shot down six enemy planes. Since then he had gone on to become a pilot himself and had been involved in many low level missions over France and Germany. Gibbs specialised in low level attacks and on one memorable occasion had destroyed a German HQ with bombs and rockets from his Mosquito fighter. In August 1944, however, he had other things on his mind - marrying his fiancé Mary Harries.

THE ESPLANADE GARDENS, PENARTH

The Esplanade, scene of great rejoicing when the lights of the Promenade were switched back on in September 1944.

On Sunday September 7th the black out in the town was replaced by a dim out and the lights on Penarth Promenade were switched on again for the first time in five years. The lights were not at full strength but they were augmented by the glow from the cafes and shops along the front. It was enough to cause great merriment in the town and groups of youths marched arm in arm along the Esplanade, singing and shouting in excitement. By the end of the first week in October, 75% of the town's electric lights were shining again. Now the end of the war was really in sight.

The town was still incurring casualties, however, as German and Japanese forces were clearly determined to fight to the bitter end. Commissioned into the South Wales Borderers, then seconded to the Kings Regiment, Captain Graham Hosegood left for India in 1941 where he went on to fight with Wingate's "Chindits" in Burma. Roaming behind enemy lines, disrupting communications and making surprise attacks on supply columns, he went missing in the summer of 1943 as his unit prepared to return to base. His Brigade Major later wrote to his parents in Penarth:-

"He was last seen fit and well at the end of March when he was starting off with a party of troops to make his way back to India, since when neither he nor any of his party has been seen."

Graham Hosegood, seen here before the war.

Graham Hosegood and his section came under fire as they were crossing the Irrawaddy River. He led his men to an island in the middle of the stream where they made a stand. Eventually, however, they were forced to surrender and spent the next eighteen months as prisoners of the Japanese.

Wingate himself wrote to Graham Hosegood's parents, Arthur and Catherine Hosegood of Clinton Road:-

"I am thankful to be able to tell you that there is definite news that your son is a prisoner in the hands of the Japanese in Burma. One cannot be 100% certain since it depends upon the evidence of escaped POWs of my force who, being Indians, are not absolutely reliable in the matter of English names, but it seems reasonably certain that Graham is alive and well - - - It gives me great pleasure to be able to tell you this. At the same time I should like to congratulate you on a very good, loyal, intelligent and devoted son. He was my Intelligence Officer and never did an IO have a more exacting job. He did it excellently well and his unfailing cheerfulness and courage were an example to all of us.
    My kind regards to you and his mother
Orde C Wingate."

Sadly Graham Hosegood died of starvation and vitamin B deficiency just three weeks before his camp in Rangoon was liberated. He had been suffering from beri-beri and lapsed into a coma from which he never recovered. His family in Penarth was expecting him home and did not hear about his death until a letter arrived from Heather Russell in India. She was a great friend of Graham's sister Joy and had assumed that the family had already been given the news. She was simply writing to express her condolences. It was a tragic way to hear the news of the death of a much loved son and a very brave man.

The grave of Captain Graham Hosegood in Rangoon War Cemetery.

In Penarth the winter of 1944-45 saw a terrific snow fall and for a while Dinas Powis was cut off, isolated from the rest of the area. The issue of housing began to be a serious concern as many of the old properties in Penarth had been damaged or destroyed by enemy bombing.

The Council applied for an allocation of the new prefabricated houses that were being set up around the country, 246 out of a total of 280 housing applicants stating that they would be prepared to accept a prefab. In the event Penarth was allocated just 50 of the new, temporary dwellings.

VE Day, when it finally came, was celebrated with great gusto, "The Penarth Times" for 10th May 1945 commenting:-

"Victory came to Penarth on Tuesday. It was the most colourful day in the history of the town. Thousands of multi-coloured flags, fluttering in the breeze from the roof-tops and the windows, symbolised the mood of the people, emerging from long years of war with Germany into peace again."

There had been an air of excitement for some days in the town as nobody knew exactly when Churchill would announce the end of hostilities. When the news finally came all the ships in the dock sounded their hooters and children danced happily along the streets. In Cogan a fancy dress parade was organised and there was dancing until midnight at the Marina Ballroom – although the building was so crowded nobody could actually move around the dance floor. All across town huge bonfires were lit, the largest being on Dock Beach. When Japan surrendered in August there were more celebrations, more bonfires, and thousands crowded onto the Esplanade. On that occasion there was dancing on the roadway and in the Italian Gardens.

Over the coming months soldiers, sailors, airmen and, in particular, POWs began to return from the war. A German U Boat, the U1023, was brought to the dock and even ventured out to sea with a party of journalists on board. Most people, however, were content to just stand and stare at this menacing war machine that had almost brought Britain to her knees.

With victory confirmed the fate of Penarth Dock once more came to the forefront of people's minds. There was no doubt that the docks had played an important part in the defeat of Nazi Germany. Figures of coal shipments for the war years show exactly how important they really were :-

1939 – 494,332 tons
1940 – 534,673 tons
1941 – 291,316 tons
1942 – 440,615 tons
1943 – 490,227 tons
1944 – 412,420 tons
1945 – 391,123 tons

These were huge figures by any standards and give a clear indication that victory was achieved not just by the fighting forces but also by the nameless thousands who worked in the shipyards, mines, factories and docks of Britain. From September 1939 until March 1945 Penarth Dock had dealt with 9,845 vessels and as well as its huge export of coal it had also handled 389,741 tons of other cargo. That meant a total tonnage through the docks of 2,826,741 tons. Now, inevitably, with hostilities ended and the country beginning to come to terms with its near-bankrupt state, Penarth Dock was surplus to requirements. Closure was most definitely on the cards once more.

For the people of Penarth it was time to take stock. At least 218 Penarth men and women died during the Second World War, among them 8 civilians. Their names were added to the town's War Memorial. Four women from the town died, compared to none at all during the

Great War – truly, war had now become total. The town's merchant seamen suffered greatly once again, no fewer than 59 of them dying while carrying out their duties.

It is interesting to see how service in the armed forces had changed by the time of the Second World War. People continued to enlist but their choice of service had changed.

During the Great War only a handful of men had served in the Royal Flying Corps or, after 1st April 1918, the RAF. It was a new arm of service and most people did not understand the strange machines they saw – or read about – stuttering into the sky. During the Second World War the RAF was a hugely popular service to join and 91 Penarth RAF men died during the six years of conflict, more Penarth casualties than in any other branch of the forces.

Five sets of brothers from the town died as well as one pairing of father and son – Evan Deere, the father, being a merchant seaman, the son Denis an Able Seaman in the Royal Navy.

Such statistics are, ultimately, quite meaningless. They cannot begin to capture the sheer tragedy of war and the way that Penarth men and women so courageously and willingly put their lives on the line in order to defend their beliefs. And in the years to come that courage would be needed several times more.

"AEROPLANE" PHOTOGRAPH
COPYRIGHT.

38A-90.

JUNKERS JU 88K, Dive Bomber.

A Junkers bomber - planes like this raided Penarth several times.

AEROFILMS SERIES

AIR VIEW OF PIER & SEA FRONT, PENARTH

29366

An aerial view of the pier.

The Garden of Remembrance.

A street party in Plassey Street to celebrate VJ Day, August 1945.

Chapter Eight – Post War Years

After the war Penarth's days as a coal exporting base were finally over. It did not mean the total closure of the docks, however, as the large expanse of water and quay space available – as well as their relatively sheltered spot beneath Penarth Head - soon proved to be ideal for the laying up and "mothballing" of ships.

The Town War Memorial.

For several years ships of the Royal Navy Reserve Fleet were moored in the docks, their machinery and armament either removed or kept serviceable by regular visits from technical staff. Minesweepers, frigates and Flower Class corvettes were kept in the dock until the late 1950s. They were not alone. The paddle steamers of P & A Campbell's White Funnel Fleet were also moored there, along with two large fully rigged sailing ships which arrived at the end of 1949.

These were the 'Passat' and 'Pamir,' old sailing ships that, at the end of the war, were due for scrapping. A West German ship-owner bought and converted them with a view to running them on a commercial basis but the enterprise proved un-economical and ownership of the two vessels passed to "The Pamir Passat Foundation" for the training of cadets. In August 1957 the 'Pamir' was lost in a hurricane in the Atlantic, over eighty officers, young trainees and crew losing their lives in the disaster. The 'Passat' also ran into difficulties that year, her cargo shifting in heavy weather and the ship having to be towed into Lisbon with a severe list to port. The training of cadets on sea-going sailing ships was promptly suspended.

Penarth Dock finally closed in 1963, most of the basin and dock area being filled in and later used for housing and light industry. The creation of a modern marina in the outer part of the old dock retains the last vestiges of the town's connection with the elements that brought the town to life in the first place.

The 'Pamir' and 'Passat,' seen here in Penarth Dock in the years after the end of the Second World War.

Penarth's involvement with the military, however, did not end with the German defeat in 1945. The ink was hardly dry on the surrender documentation before the people of Britain – many of them still serving in the forces – voted Churchill out of office and brought in a new Labour Government. Conscription had never been popular in Britain but it had been an essential factor in both World Wars. As far as the British people were concerned, compulsory service in the armed forces during peacetime was unknown and decidedly unwelcome.

The Garden of Remembrance.

Clement Attlee, the new Prime Minister, was personally opposed to conscription but he had promised to quickly bring home the troops who had fought the war – that was part of the election manifesto that had seen him win what is now known as the "khaki election." And yet Britain had still to carry out its share of policing trouble spots across the globe and helping shattered communities find their feet again. Despite his better judgement,

"I was often subjected to their humour, like everyone else, I suppose. But my name gave them a real chance to show their wit – 'What's your name, boy?' 'Howell, Corporal.' 'I'll make you howl! Get in the Tin Room!' The Tin Room was where all the pots and pans for cooking were kept and washed."

Ken served mainly in Northern Ireland, with breaks of a few months here and there, between 1982 and 2000. It was at the height of the Irish Troubles and he was involved with maintaining and repairing the helicopters of 72 Squadron. Three incidents, in particular, stick in his mind. During routine operations over the "Bandit Country" of South Armagh, the helicopters used to land on farmland outside Belfast and the farm dog would regularly attack their tail rotors and fins. On one occasion there were even teeth marks in the metal, the dog having hung on for dear life as the helicopter rose into the air. The second memory could have had a tragic end:-

"The Sealink Ferry 'Antrim Princess' had some engine trouble off the Antrim coast and we went out to help. A crewman on board the ship fired a rocket line at the helicopter and scored a direct hit. The line wrapped around the tail rotor, making control of the helicopter very difficult. It only just made it to the cliff top for an emergency landing."

The last memory is, perhaps, a bit of light relief:-

"We were on surveillance flights, hovering, surveying the buildings and general area. There had been a heavy snowfall and I remember a woman coming out with a kettle of boiling water. She used the water to write a message in the snow. You can imagine what she wrote – let's just say the last word was 'off.'"

When he left the RAF in 2000, after 39 years service, Ken Howell returned to the town he had always loved. Now, in retirement, he acts as a voluntary caseworker for the Royal British Legion in Penarth.

Argentina invaded the Falkland Islands on 2nd April 1982 and the event sparked off a wave of indignation throughout the country. Bill Aspinall, later to become Registrar of Births, Deaths and Marriages at West House in Penarth, was Colour Sergeant with the Royal Marines garrison in Stanley at the time of the invasion. He had joined the Marines in 1961, served in places like Singapore and Malaya, seen action in Borneo and covered the British withdrawal from Aden. He was drafted to the Falklands in February 1982:-

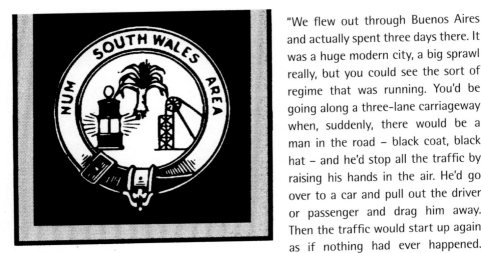

"We flew out through Buenos Aires and actually spent three days there. It was a huge modern city, a big sprawl really, but you could see the sort of regime that was running. You'd be going along a three-lane carriageway when, suddenly, there would be a man in the road – black coat, black hat – and he'd stop all the traffic by raising his hands in the air. He'd go over to a car and pull out the driver or passenger and drag him away. Then the traffic would start up again as if nothing had ever happened. The inflation in the country was astronomical and you could sense the Government would have to do something to stop it. We didn't know then, of course, that what they'd do was invade the Falklands."

The Marines first realised that something untoward was going on after the incident of the scrap dealers on South Georgia was made public. Then, about ten days before the invasion, an Argentinean Hercules sent out a Mayday call and made a forced landing on the Stanley air strip. Within a few hours it had been miraculously repaired and had taken off – the Argentineans now knew they could land a Hercules in the Falklands. Bill Aspinall was told about 4.00pm on 1st April that an invasion was imminent:-

"We spent the night preparing. We had just sent off a detachment on the 'Endurance' so we were under-manned. They'd also taken our only working mortar with them so it wasn't a very comfortable thought, knowing that all we had was small arms. We made our dispositions and managed to get some sleep about 4.00am and then things started to happen. We got a radio message from a bloke out in the Sound, saying there were some big ships all around him. Within a few minutes we came under small arms fire. The Argies had landed."

Bill and his men were positioned around Government House and for the next twelve hours were engaged in a fierce fire fight. None of the Marines were killed but three Argentinean soldiers were shot dead and three more taken prisoner. The Falkland Island locals were told to stay indoors, out of the way, but it was a message that was often misunderstood or ignored:-

"In the middle of the fire fight, bullets flying everywhere, I got a message from one of my men – 'Colours,' he said, 'I've got a bloke here on a bike, says he wants to get to work.' I couldn't believe it. 'Tell him to go home,' I said. 'Doesn't he know there's a war going on?' We did have one local man, part of the Falklands Islands Defence Force – a bit like the TA units back home – and, fair play to him, he stayed with us the whole time. Late on in the afternoon a huge Armoured Personnel Carrier, armed with Browning machine guns, came trundling up the road towards us. It was followed by several more. I remember thinking 'That's it, we're stuffed now.'"

As dusk fell the Argentinean forces called a truce and asked to talk with the Governor, Rex Hunt. The Marines were ready to slip away into Stanley and fight from house to house but Hunt did not want the locals endangered in any way and decided to surrender. The Marines were put on an aeroplane and taken, via Buenos Aires, to Montevideo in Uruguay. And there Bill Aspinall could not believe what he found:-

"They put us into this amazing 5 Star hotel. We had no money as we'd had to leave with just what we stood up in but after a while we were told we could sign for anything we wanted, food, drink, whatever, and the bills would be sorted out later. Well, I tell you, Mrs Thatcher and Queen Victoria had never signed for so many receipts in their lives!"

Bill was sent back to the UK but within a few weeks was on his way south again. He caught up with the Task Force in the Ascension Islands and, promoted now to Warrant Officer, fought throughout the relieving campaign. He was part of the spearhead that took Mt Harriet and Mt Juliet before sailing home on the 'Canberra.':-

"The only thing that worried me was the fact that, if I'd been taken prisoner, they could have shot me. After all, I'd been a prisoner of war and wasn't really supposed to be fighting again. We sailed for home in July '82. That return trip on the 'Canberra' will stay with me for ever. During the voyage the 'Broadsword' came alongside – and remember, we were still in the South Atlantic, on black out – and suddenly all her lights were on. The full crew was lined up on deck and they saluted the Royal Marine commandoes, hats in the air, just like you see in the pictures. I tell you, it sent the hairs up on the back of my neck. And then, of course, the ticker-tape welcome in Southampton – lights on the headland, hooters going off, flotillas of small boats, well it was just incredible."

Several Penarth men fought in the Falklands campaign, including Paul Evans who served with the RAF Regiment and Francoise Slingerland of the Royal Engineers. When Arthur Smith, who served on board the 'Invincible,' came home he was greeted by a poem in "The Penarth Times":-

"They sent Harriers and jump jets
And many a hit was scored
By the lads from the 'Invincible'
Till the Argies had been floored.
Galtieri knew he was beaten
And with anger roared
'Caramba! Give them back Malvinas,
They've got Arthur Smith on board.'"

The poem was written by Mrs Gorlay, a neighbour of Arthur's parents, and the sense of pride in the achievements of all of the town's warriors can be clearly seen.

In May 1982 Sir Edward Youde, who had been born in Penarth, was made the Governor of Hong Kong. Youde had lived in Mountjoy Avenue until he was 17 years old and was third secretary at the British Embassy in Nanking during the famous Yangste Incident of 1949. With the British frigate 'Amethyst' trapped by Communist troops, Youde trekked along the river for four days to appeal to the Communists to give the frigate safe passage. Although his plea was rejected and the frigate had to run the gauntlet of Chinese Communist guns, his mission was said to have eased the general situation.

When Saddam Hussein invaded Kuwait in 1990 Bombadier Gareth Dibble of Penarth was part of the 9000 strong Armoured Brigade that was sent to the Gulf to assist in chasing the dictator and his forces back to Iraq. The deadline for Saddam to withdraw his forces passed on 15th January 1991 and battle duly commenced. In February Gareth Dibble was writing about his experiences:-

"the campaign is in its 14th day, with the Allied air bombardment continuing and I can hear planes flying over, heading north towards Kuwait for another sortie. All in all the morale amongst the men is exceptionally high. The attitude is 'The sooner we get the job done, the sooner we go home.'"

Other Penarth men with the army in the Gulf that year were people like Lee Restell and Kevin Cooper. Mark Bow was serving on board HMS 'Atherstone,' a Hunt Class minesweeper.

She was the first British warship to head for the Gulf when war broke out and spent the campaign clearing mines from the shipping lanes.

Penarth sea front on a wild and wet winter day.

One of the most notable things about Penarth servicemen is the degree of continuity they provide. There are soldiers serving now who have had fathers and even grandfathers in the forces before them. Gunner Sam Chick is one example. His grandfather and uncles served in the Great War and the Second World War and the Chick name features prominently on the Great War section of the town War Memorial.

At the time of writing Sam Chick is serving with the Royal Horse Artillery supplying armed support for the 7th Parachute Regiment in Afghanistan. He also served in Iraq during the second Gulf War and, operating light field guns, his unit was often pushed out ahead of the infantry:-

"Our guns didn't have the range of the Iraqi weapons, so that's why we had to get out ahead. We had a lot of in-coming for a few days. We cut the Basra/Baghdad line and they didn't like that very much so they had quite a pop at us. My mate got shot in the backside – I remember the medics arguing whether to stitch him inside or outside first. It certainly made us laugh."

Since being sent to Afghanistan Gunner Sam Chick has seen more action. He is clear that the Afghans present a much more serious obstacle than the Iraqis:-

"It's a bit like the Wild West out there. They're good fighters, the Afghans, always have been. Our Regimental Battle Honours include the First and Second Afghan Wars. We had a battery wiped out in the first war and the guns weren't recaptured until the second one. Now they're just as tough. They're certainly not scared to stand up and fight us. One of my mates was shot in the chest and the bullet bounced off his spine before exiting through his arm. He was so lucky, it missed every vital organ in his body. "

Sam Chick loves his life in the army. He has another 17 years to serve and is clear that there is nothing else he would rather do for a living.

SAPPER
CHARLES HUBERT HALLETT
454541
ROYAL ENGINEERS
2/4 FIELD COMPANY
GLAMORGAN FORTRESS COMPANY
1915-1918

Sapper Hubert Hallett, just one in a long line of Penarth men who served their country in times of need.

Elgan Hallett is another serviceman from a long line of Penarth soldiers. His great uncle, Sapper Charles Hallett, served in the Great War, surviving the conflict to finish up as a journalist in south- east England. His grandfather, Cyril Hallett, was in Egypt with the RAF during the Second World War. At the time of writing, Elgan is serving in the RAF as an Avionics Technician with 28 (AC) Squadron in Iraq:-

"We work with up to seven Merlin Mk 3 helicopters, repairing and maintaining them. The helicopters are used for various operations, everything from transporting troops and catching insurgents or militia to providing immediate response cover for casualties. As engineers and ground crew we can work in anything up to 50 degrees centigrade in the summer months. Then, in winter, temperatures will drop to almost freezing during the night, a maximum of 30 degrees during the day."

Elgan Hallett served in the aftermath of the first Gulf War, in Saudi Arabia and is clear that he enjoys his life in the RAF. It is a job he has been trained to do, one that he will carry out until the end of his enlistment.

Penarth as it should be remembered, in evening sunlight.

The message is simple. Penarth men and women have always served their country and their community. From the early days of the town in the 1860s, right up until the present day, they have willingly and consistently put their lives on the line in times of danger and crisis. They will undoubtedly continue to do so in the years ahead. That, more than anything else, is the real story of Penarth.

Conclusion

Penarth is a unique community, fostered out of the need to first build and then run a dock to export Welsh coal. When the coal dried up so, too, did the need for the docks. Yet the town continued to thrive, creating a niche for itself as a seaside resort and as a dormitory town for nearby Cardiff.

Penarth has no magnificent architecture and no world-shattering deeds took place within its confines. It is the people of the town that make it special. This book has tried to tell their story – or at least a part of it. No book of 35,000 words can ever hope to catch the real essence of the place and its people. Arguably, no book, regardless of its size, can ever achieve that. This work does not claim to be a full and complete history of the town and its people. It is, quite simply, a snap shot, a brief glimpse of just some of the characters who lived – and still live – in the town. There are many others and readers who know of them may well lament their exclusion. The choice of people to include had been arbitrary, depending as much upon the author's interests and enthusiasms as much as anything else. If that is a fault then it is mine.

The stories and the people presented here are, by turns, tragic and sad, funny and illuminating. They are part of the microcosm that invariably goes to make up a community. Most of the people mentioned here will never achieve immortality on a world stage yet they have carried out amazing deeds and seen amazing things. They are part of the wonderful story of Penarth.

Penarth, as a living, thriving environment, continues to grow and develop. Its full story has still to be told but that will not happen, I hope, for a long time yet. When everything has finally been said and done, when the total story has at last been told, the town will be dead, as empty as one of those Wild West ghost towns that movie makers seem to love. Penarth is better than that. Penarth will live on.

And so, really, the full story of the town will never be told. That has to be its finest legacy.

Appendix 1

The following list of the town's dead has been taken from Penarth War Memorial. It is not complete. As we have seen, other Penarth men and women have died in conflict and are not commemorated here. The list contains only the names of people who died in the Great War and the Second World War – and even then, there may well be names missing. If so, the author apologises for any omissions and would welcome any information so that amendments might be made for any future editions of this volume.

The Great War

D Abbott, A F Aberg, R Absalom, W Adams, D Andrews, E M Angove, F M Aubrey, S D Aubrey, E W Bartlett, F A Bartlett, H A Bartlett, R Bendon, W J Bennett, E Beresford, J Bickle, H S Bird, J W Black, F Blackmore, J O Boole, D Bousie, C E Bowen, E Boyle, Jack Boyle, John Boyle, A N Brown, R W Buck, W Buckland, P Buckley, T W J Burge, FH Burge, W G Burge, A Cann, W N Carey-Thomas, A G Carr, H Clamen, A Chick, E Chick, H M Clements, R V Cleaves, A W Clive, W Cole, C Collins, R Coney, W H Coney, F Cook, H A Cooper, S Cosslett, S C Cousins, T H Cox, A E Coyle, S Crane, F R Crimp, C Crowden, E J Culliford, F Dakers, D V Davies, E T Davies, G L Davies, S Davies, W H Davies, W J Davies, E W Davies, E Davison, H Davison, W C Dawe, H C De Claire, E F Denman, C W Downs, J Driscol, L W P East, A Edwards, R Ellis, W H Ellis, W Ernest, H Essery, H P Evans, J R Evans, T P Evans, D Farquhar Thompson, H O Fitzgerald, O Fitzgerald, T Fitzgerald, B J T Flack, W H Flack, W Foot, O J H Foote, L J M Francis, W J A Fry, I Gall, G H Gallagher, W R Gambling, W J Garland, R Garwood, G Gibbon, J A Gibbs, T A Gibson, F J A Gillham, J N Gillies, F Goddard, E Goodfellow, J Gough, S J Gould, A E Gray, P Gribble.

W H Griffiths, H A Gunn, G R Guy, H L Hall, H E Hall, G O Hammond, J W Hand, S Harris, F C Harry, C J Hart, A J Hartrey, A Harvey, E Hayes,, C C Heywood, H Hill, J E Hills, E C Hookway, F H Hooper, H C Hooper, W Hooper, C R Hort, D G Hoult, P C Hoult,, R A Hoult, A Howard, G O Howell, A W E Howells, F H Howells, F Howells, J H Hughes, O J Hughes, E A Hunt, A E Hutchings, H Iles, E L James, R L James, C H Jeffcot, T Jefferies, A G Jenkins, C G Jenkins, T Jenkins, R John, T H Johnson, G E Johnston, G J C Jolliffe, A Jones, A T Jones, C L J Jones, G Jones, H Jones, T Jones, T Keegan, J Kenny, C Kenure, W H Lamperd, W G Langford, W M Lee, A E Legg, T J Lewis, W H Lewis, F Lingham, H Livermore, H P Lloyd, W G Loader, F C Lock, G R Lougher, G H Love, J B Lye, C H Macdonald, G Maddocks, H C Maidment, E S Martyn, C Matthews, G E Matthews, E E C Maunder, F J G Maunder, T W Maunder, A C Meadows, S Middleton, W Middleton, A S Monroe, W Monroe, A Morgan, G V Morgan, E Morris, F Morris,

H Morris, A Mules, I Mules, E Murray, J Murray, D F Oakes, E Palfrey, R Palfrey, W R Parkman, E J Parry, R J Pawley, A Payne, I I Pearce, R Pearce, D St Pettigrew, Emily A Pickford, R G Pike, F G Pope, T A Powell, T J Powell, I Prideux, C P Probert.

W R Radford, A H Reed, E L Rees, J T Rees, J Regan, S Reynolds, F C Richards, J J Richards, P W Richards, P H Rixon, A V Rowley, G R Sandrey, T H Sandrey, O G Sanger, J Searle, T H Shute, A C Sims, E B Smailes, F G Smith, R E Smith, S J M Spear, S J Spear, S Spear, B Spence, A V Spiller, G H Stickler, W A Sweet-Escott, A N Tait, A Talbot, T Taylor, A Thomas, A J Thomas, B J Thomas, C HR Thomas, J Rhys Thomas, John R Thomas, R J Thomas, R P Thomas, Richard Thomas, S Thomas, W H Thomas, W Hugh-Thomas, A Thompson, H Thompson, T Thorne, W G Tongs, L Townsend, A Tregaskis, L Tregaskis, F Trump, C W Tucker, W J Tunley, F W G A Uden, B H Vyvyan, C Vyvyan-Robinson, H S Wakeford, R S Wakeford, E K Walker, F J Wall, F Ward, G Ware, W T Watkins, A Watts, J Weaver, G Webber, M Webber, A J West, G H Westecott, G F Wehrley, E C Whiley, C White, H D White, H J White, A Whitley, F L Whittington, G Widdowfield, J Wiggins, A C Williams, C E H Williams, C Williams, J C Williams, J L Williams, J H Williams, T J Williams, G Wilson, K P Window, L C R Window, H Wride, G H Wright, H E Wynne-Williams, C De C Yeld, C A Young, W Young, C S J Yule.

The Second World War

C Adamson, E C Allen, J W Allsopp, A Andrews, A Ashcroft, C Ashcroft, J A Ashley, J H Baker, S Baker, R Barrett, F Bartlett, T A C Beddoe, L Beer, D A V Beer, J H Bendon.

R Berry, J Biggs, W H Bohlen, R M Bond, H H Bowden, L Bowmer, V G Brailey, L J Brice, S J Brix, J I Brown, E J Browning, A Buckley, A Bulmer, H B Burn, E Clarke, E W Coates, A M Cole, F E Cole, D H Connibear, J Cotterill, P W Crocker, T D Crockett, G W Cox, J R Cox, G H Crowther, B Cumming, R J Curtin, R S T Dalgleish, P D Davidson, T L Davies, W C Dawson, G Dean, D P Deare, E Deere, D P Dennison, A E J Dentton, D C Dewar, J S Dicker, P D Doorly, S C Draper, S drew, R C Edwards, T W Eley, K Elliot, A C Emery, D G England, A J Evans, F A Evans, H N G Evans, W T Evans, A A Facey, K Farnden, S J Fish, F G Ford, P Ford, W Fox, H Frank, A E Fricker, A E Gambling, D Garrett, M J C Garrett, G P Gibson, T Gilderdale.

L Godfrey, W Goodyear, T R Gould, F G Greenaway, H M G Griffiths, R E Gunter, F C Guy, Dorothy P Gye, J Hale, A Hall, W H Halls, D Harkin, G J Hayes, H Hayes, F Heap, W H Heap, R L Heath, R A H Herbert, G Henslop, F H Hooper, A Hopkins, H P Hopkins, G C Hosegood, E Hunt, H Hunt, F Hutchings, A G James, R James, A Jenkins, T E Jenkins, W J P John, F W Jones, F Jones, H R Jones, L C J Jones, R E Jones, R Jones, F J Joshua, N Kean, J Kennedy, M H King, A Kipling, D L Kitchener, Jane Kulke, P H Lansdale, L Lawday, R J Lee,, C Leeds, J Llewellyn,

R T Lougher, G Lovegrove, W Mahoney, N Marshall, R J Martin, W Martin, E Mathews, A C Matthews, F G Matthews, P F Matthews, R C McClement, E J McIver, A McLoud, E Middleton, F W Moates, A J Morgan, D Morgan, J Morgan, J R D Morgan, R Morgan, C J Morgan, J Murray, H Neale, F Nelson, J S M Nicholls, E J Oakes, W Oakey.

R Oakley, C W Ollson, C M Owen, J T Parry, A J Pearce, C N Petherick, H J Phillips, R F Poole, F Reed, T L Roberts, H Rooney, H N Ross, D Scott, P L Scott, L W Sewell, R F Silver, T Simcoe, R Slimmings, H G Smith, S Smith, W Smith, R Stevenson, H Storey, L C Strachen, R K Street, D Sutherland, H H Sutton, J E Swain, H S Thomas, H M Thomas, M J Thomas, R P Thomas, J P Thompson, L Thompson, B G Tillyard, H D Tongs, E J Turnbull, J E Turner, W J Turner, A G Venn, J A Venn, J E Vieren, F W Vodden, C H Walker, C H Walter, R W Walters, K A Warwick, T G Watson, Margaret H Weight, P Wenger, G H Whalley, R C Whittington, B T Williams, C W Williams, H S Pardoe-Williams, P T Williams, H W Woodhouse, H Woods, J S Young, W Young, M H McCarthy, A L Swaine, J A Huish.

Civilian Casualties

B Clemerson, F Cox, Jane Cox, G Davies, D J Evans, A E Matthews, Sarah Elizabeth Matthews, Kathleen Morgan.

Appendix II

Penarth Memorials

This list of memorials in Penarth has been taken from "Penarth Area War Memorial Transcripts" by Marcus Payne. They are the result of his indefatigable efforts. The list presented here is not complete but covers only the main memorials – for a full list see Marcus Payne's transcript in Penarth Library.

There are very few memorials to individual soldiers in Britain dating to the period before the Boer War. Penarth is no different from the rest of the country and the interested browser or historian will look long and hard to find any mention of dead soldiers before 1914. Similarly, there seem to be precious few memorials to the dead of the Korean War, the Falklands campaign and so on:-

Memorials/Cenotaphs

Penarth War Memorial – Alexandra Park
The Garden of Remembrance – Alexandra Park
Roll of Honour – St Augustine's Church
Stained glass window – Royal British Legion
War Memorial Screen – All Saints Church
Memorial stone cross – Trinity Church

Buildings

Headlands School (previously the J A Gibbs Home)
Memorial Grandstand at Penarth Rugby Club

Plaques

Albert Road Methodist Church
Glamorganshire Golf Club
Stanwell School
Holy Nativity Church
Penarth Yacht Club
Stanwell Road Baptist Chapel
Masonic Hall
Trinity Church

A number of individual memorials and gravestones exist at St Augustine's Church and in the town cemetery.

Bibliography

Secondary Sources:

E Alwyn Benjamin   "Penarth 1841-71," Pub by D Brown & Sons, 1980

Geoffrey Bennett   "Coronel and the Falklands," Pub by Batsford, 1962

Paul Brickhill   "The Dam Busters," Pub by Evans Bros, 1951

Phil Carradice   "A History of Headlands School," M Ed Thesis, Cardiff 1989
"Penarth: The Story, Vol 1," Penarth Press, 2004

K Cooper and J E Davies   "The Cardiff Pals," Pub by Militia Cymraeg, 1998

M N Duffy   "The Twentieth Century," London 1964

David Fanning   "St Joseph's, Penarth," Pub by Hallmark, 1990

Niall Ferguson   "The Pity of War," Pub by Allen Laine, 1998

Paul Fussell   "The Great War and Modern Memory," Pub by OUP, 1975

John and Sheila Gibbs   "Trinity Methodist Church: A Portrait," London 1994

Tom Hickman   "The Call Up," Pub by Headline, 2004

David Ings   "Penarth in Old Picture Postcards," Vol 1 & 2, European Library 1990

Mike Irwin   "Victoria's Cross," Australia, 2003

Neil Oliver   "Not Forgotten," Pub by Hodder and Stoughton, 2005

Marcus Payne	"Penarth Area War Dead Biographies, 1914-1919, Penarth, 2004
	"Penarth Area War Dead Biographies, 1939-1946, Penarth, 2004
	"Penarth Area War Memorials Transcripts," Penarth 2002-04
Robert Phillips	"The Battle of Mametz Wood 1916," Aberystwyth, undated
Michael Steadman	"Great Battles of the Great War," Pub by Leo Cooper, 1999
Alan Thorne	"Place Names of Penarth," D Brown & Sons, 1997
Roy Thorne	"A History of Penarth Dock," Unpublished Thesis, 1984
	"Penarth: A History," Vol 1 & 2, Starling Press, 1975

Primary Sources:

The Penarth Times
The Penarth Observer
The Penarth News
The Cardiff Times
Penarth Parish Magazine, Jan – Dec 1916
Highways and Hedges (NCH magazine)

Phil Carradice is a poet, novelist and historian. He has written over 30 books, including the highly successful "Penarth: The Story Vol 1." He is a regular broadcaster on BBC Radio Wales and is a noted teacher of creative writing.